First published 1995

ISBNs: 0-9526051-0-4

C.K. Publisher,
33 The Stour,
Grange Estate,
Daventry,
Northamptonshire,
NN11 4PR.

GH00703219

Food Preparation by Donna Grove
Typeset by Matthew Searle
Art and Design by Michael Clarke
Edited by Edwin Baris
Photography by Ken Walker

Printed and bound in Great Britain by:

Print X-Press (UK) Ltd.,
Morris Road,
Royal Oak Industrial Estate,
Daventry,
Northamptonshire,
NN11 5PD.

COOK MALAYSIAN STYLE

By Caroline Knight

ACKNOWLEDGEMENTS

I would like to express my gratitude to my aunt, Mrs Khang Hang Poh and my brother Mr Chuah Teik Sun for all the support and encouragement they have given and the generous contribution of their recipes which has assisted in the writing of this book.

Thanks to both my best friends, Mrs Lily Loh and Mrs Patricia Teng, for booking accommodation for me in July 1994 and giving me their recipes.

I would also like to thank my son Marco Grove and my daughter Donna Grove for their help with the photography, Jess Oakes for her editorial help and advice and all the girls at Daventry Tertiary College for their assistance, with special thanks to:

- Sharron Bell
- Diane Osborne
- Jane Carvell
- Marisa Rushton
- Liz Bamforth
- Maggie Carthew
- Ann Walker
- Janet Hutchinson
- Angela Tyrell

DEDICATION

To my dearest brother Chuah Teik Sun,
my daughter Donna Grove,
my son Marco Grove
and Roy with all my love.

COOK MALAYSIAN STYLE
BY
CAROLINE KNIGHT

INTRODUCTION

The aim of my book is to give everyone a chance to try out these authentic, ancient Malayan dishes. The recipes within contain original flavours with pungent, mild and spicy tastes, some food is cooked with coconut milk.

During the early 15th century traders from India, China, Portugal and Holland arrived at the port of Malacca, which was and is a still trading centre. The Portuguese took the power from Malayan hands in 1511. By 1641 the Dutch took over Malacca and in 1795, it changed hands yet again, when the British took control. The British were interested in the sea-ports and trade routes, and also interested in tin mines as well as rubber plantations.

In 1963 the north states of Borneo which is Sabah and Sarawak joined Malaya and also Singapore. It was then called "Malaysia" but Singapore pulled out within a short time. Timber is economic in Sabah, while pepper , cacao and oil comes from Sarawak.

Malaya had its Independence from Britain in 1957. Chinese and Indian traders stayed behind at Malacca, except the Europeans. So these men settled down and got married to local women. The three major races of Malaya are Chinese, Malay and Indian. Each of them have their own cultures. Rice is mainly eaten everyday. The spices used are similar. The Chinese use spices like star-anise, blachan (prawn-paste), lemon-grass, yellow ginger, chilli and coconut, while the Malays use lemon-grass, chilli, tamarind juice, coconut and yellow ginger. The Indians use fresh curry paste like chilli, yellow ginger, cardamon-pods, coriander and cummin seeds. We don't weigh our ingredients like the British. We just have a pinch of this and that, but measurements are given at the back of the book to help you.

In each state of Malaya they have their own special taste. Their cuisines are delicious, it makes you feel hungry just looking at the food.

One of the world's favourite dishes is "Satay" which is chicken or beef barbecued over a charcoal fire, served with cucumber, rice cake, cucumber and peanut sauce. Laksa is another popular Malay dish - noodles cooked in a spicy chilli sauce. Mee-Jawa is noodles cooked in a thick gravy sauce served with prawn fritters, potato slices and tofu (bean-curd).

One of the most popular Chinese dishes is "Chicken Rice" which is cooked in chicken stock served with chicken, roast pork and cucumber slices. Another favourite is "Hokkien-Mee" which is egg noodles cooked in prawn sauce served with prawns, pork slices, green vegetables and bean sprouts, and sprinkled with crispy brown onions. Penang "LAKSA" is a very popular dish too. It is white rice noodles cooked in spicy fish gravy, served with pineapple, cucumber and garnished with sprigs of mint leaves.

The most popular Indian dish is "Murtabak" which is a thin pastry filled with egg, meat and vegetables. Another one is "Roti-chenan" which is pan-cake fried and served with curry sauce. Mee-goreng is another snack which is egg noodles fried with spicy chilli paste, served with prawns, tofu (bean-curd), egg and tomato. Ice Kachang is a dessert made of crushed ice served with ice-cream, jelly, fruits and three types of syrups.

There are many Indian, Chinese and Malayan restaurants everywhere. Even coffee shops sell a lot of local food. There is a wide variety to choose from to suit all tastes. You can find hawkers selling food on every street corner. People in Malaya find it cheaper to eat out rather than cook at home.

To the north-east of Malaya lies the state of Kedah which is known as the "Rice Bowl" of Malaya. It grows enough rice to feed the whole population. When you drive through Kedah you can see paddy fields on both sides of the road. There are acres and acres of them. There is an old Chinese saying, "You must not leave any rice behind on your plate or else you'll be poor later".

In the early days of the Straits Settlement of Malaya in the 15th Century, the Chinese women were known as "Nonyas" , because at that time, Malay men married Chinese women. Now they are called the "Straits Chinese". The Nonyas are very old fashioned and they like to perfume their meat and vegetables. They wear a bun with a hairpin through the hair. They also wear a lace top and a sarong. They use fingers to eat rather than spoons and forks. All mothers teach their daughters how to cook the proper way in the kitchen. Most of the food is still cooked by the same-old fashioned method, with techniques nearly the same today as they were then. However some have changed to a more modern method of cooking.

I attended a re-union party with my school friends the last time I went home to Malaya. I was pleasantly surprised to find that we were all able to contact each other again after all these years.

The meals my friends cooked were truly excellent; vast quantities of satisfying, mouth watering food, and so delicious that I couldn't wait to try out the recipes myself. I hope that you will do the same!

My aunt, who is a very good cook, knows when I'm coming home, and invites me to her home where she takes a lot of trouble cooking the food. She loves cooking just like me. My mother used to work as a cook for a very rich family, and also loves cooking. My brother used to run his own food business. So naturally I take after my mother, who explained everything to me, from beginning to end. I try to remember everything she said and I find it fascinating. One of my favourite dishes is curry fish cooked in tamarind juice served with rice. It has a sweet and sour flavour. Prawn fritters is also another of my favourites. Spare-ribs cooked in soya-sauce with mushroom and egg is another tasty dish.

In Penang at Esplanade, which is on the sea-front, there is a big open air area where traders sell a wide variety of local food in the evening. Another place is called Guerney Drive, another big eating place, with a twice weekly night market. The market sells everything from pots and pans to clothes and music. Even in Penang Road there are quite a few stalls selling local food which is very cheap, about £1.50 per person including drinks. There is absolutely no shortage of hawkers and food stalls. How about taking a ride in a trishaw on a guided tour around Georgetown?. It will cost you less than $15.00 Malayan Dollars (which is £4.00 English money). Everybody is very helpful and friendly.

Now you know a little about my country past and present, why not try my country's recipes.

HAPPY COOKING! *Caroline Knight*

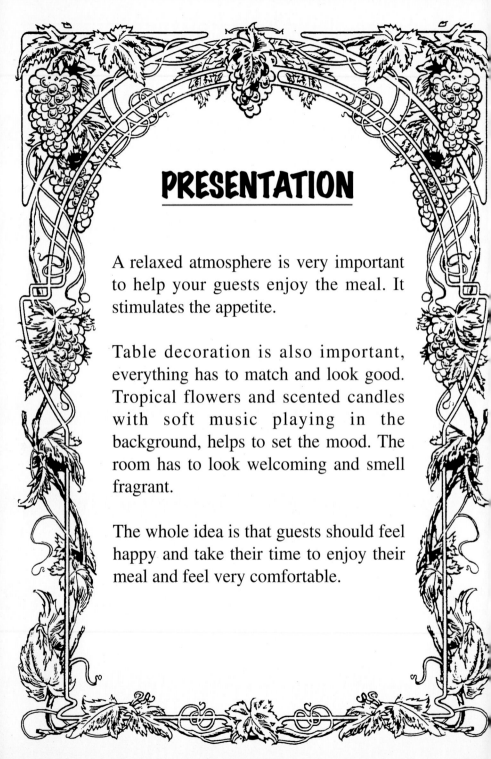

PRESENTATION

A relaxed atmosphere is very important to help your guests enjoy the meal. It stimulates the appetite.

Table decoration is also important, everything has to match and look good. Tropical flowers and scented candles with soft music playing in the background, helps to set the mood. The room has to look welcoming and smell fragrant.

The whole idea is that guests should feel happy and take their time to enjoy their meal and feel very comfortable.

CONTENTS

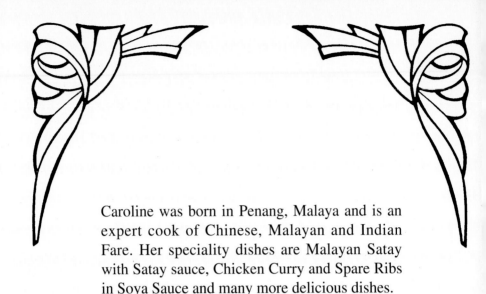

Caroline was born in Penang, Malaya and is an expert cook of Chinese, Malayan and Indian Fare. Her speciality dishes are Malayan Satay with Satay sauce, Chicken Curry and Spare Ribs in Soya Sauce and many more delicious dishes.

She enjoys cooking and entertaining her guests and gets immense satisfaction from the comments of her guests; who sometimes give her new ideas for future dishes. For many years she has been collecting recipes from her mother, relations and friends and dreaming that one day she would collate together and write a book.

Please try out these dishes in her book, I know you will get immense pleasure not only in preparation, but eating them as well.

Good luck and happy cooking.

Equipment: Wok, bamboo steamer, rice cooker, pestle and mortar.

PENANG FRIED RICE

Serves 4
4 cups rice
1 large onion (peeled and sliced)
2 to 3 tablespoons vegetable oil
1 to 2 tablespoons sesame oil
1/2 lb (225 gm) Lean pork (seasoned
   with salt and pepper)
1/2 lb (225 gm) prawns

2 tablespoons dark soya sauce
1 tablespoon sweet soya sauce
1 Chinese sausage (finely sliced)
1 medium carrot (peeled and finely sliced)
4 oz peas
2 large eggs

For garnish: Sprinkle a few drops of sweet chilli sauce (optional)
Finely slice 2 onions and deep-fry until golden brown and crispy.
2 fresh red chillies, finely sliced and 1 tablespoon light soya sauce.

METHOD:

Wash and boil the rice in a saucepan on medium heat for about 25 minutes until fluffy.
Adding more water if necessary during cooking. When rice is cooked, remove from heat.
Wash the pork and pat dry with paper towel. Cut pork into small pieces. Finely slice the
onions and the sausage. Heat the vegetable and the sesame oil together in the wok until
quite hot on medium heat, add the onions and stir fry until light brown, about 2 minutes.

Then add the pork and stir for 3 to 4 minutes. Add the rice and stir well for 5 minutes. Add
prawns, Chinese sausage, peas and carrots and stir for a further 5 minutes. Add soya sauce
and continue stirring. Pour a little oil into the centre of the wok and crack the eggs into
the oil and then stir the rice until well mixed. Transfer rice into a large serving dish and
garnish with crispy fried onions. Also serve with a side dish of red sliced chillies with light
soya sauce, or add sweet chilli sauce to taste.

POH FUN - CANTONESE STYLE RICE

Serves 4
4 cups of rice
4 chicken breasts (cut into small pieces)
4 cups of water
4 cloves garlic (chopped)
10 Chinese mushrooms (soaked in water
   until soft,drained and finely sliced)
3 tablespoons oyster sauce

2 tablespoons dark soya sauce
1 Chinese sausage (finely sliced)
1 inch fresh ginger (2.5 cm) finely sliced
1 tablespoon sugar
1/2 teaspoon aji-no-moto (Gourmet Powder)
A pinch of salt

METHOD:

Boil the rice in a deep saucepan with 4 cups of water for about 15 minutes. Do not use too
much water when boiling the rice. Next add chicken pieces and stir well.

Then add all the other ingredients, oyster sauce, soya sauce, mushrooms, sausages, and stir until well mix. Cook for a further 10 minutes so that the rice finish off cooking and then remove it from heat and stir again. It should look soft, fluffy and brown. Serve while it is hot.

TIPS:

Rice is normally cooked in a clay pot with the chicken, but any saucepan will do.

NASI KUNYIT (YELLOW RICE)

Nasi Kunyit" is known as "Yellow Rice" in Malay. This rice is called "Glutinous Rice" which is used for puddings and cakes. The rice is normally soaked in water overnight, enlarging it to swell and become soft in texture. The following day, the rice is steamed on a tray in a steamer. During the steaming process, the juice of yellow ginger is sprinkled onto the rice along with the coconut milk and once it is well mixed, it is then covered with a lid to finish off steaming. In Malaya "Nasi Kunyit" is used for a very special occasion, for example when a baby is born after 4 weeks old, during celebration a large amount of "Nasi Kunyit" is cooked with chicken curry and some other cakes. The baby's parents would deliver food to their relations and friends. In return they received one dozen eggs, longlife noodles and a red packet which contains money for the baby.

cups Glutinous Rice (uncooked)
pieces Kunyit (turmeric) Ground finely and mix with 3 tablespoons of water then drain.
cup of Coconut Milk (thick)
Banana Leaves or use foil

METHOD:

Wash the rice and drain, then mix thoroughly with the Kunyit, leave it overnight.
The best time to prepare it is in the evening so that it is ready to be cooked the following day.
Line a basket for steaming with a thin piece of white cloth and place the rice in it.
Steam the rice on a very slow heat, by using a wok half filled with water. Make sure the water does not run dry, check frequently.
While the rice is being cooked sprinkle in the coconut milk, a little at a time until the rice is cooked.
Remove the rice from the basket and put on to a plate. Press the rice between the banana leaves until the rice sticks firmly together and is flat.
Nasi Kunyit is a yellow powder spice known as "Turmeric", which is a ginger. It is also called "yellow rice", when it is cooked it is normally eaten with chicken or beef curry.

MEE GORENG (INDIAN STIR FRIED NOODLE)

Mee Goreng is a very tasty Indian stir fried egg noodle , which can be eaten anytime as a snack.
It can be served with:

Beancurd slices, Lettuce, Prawns or Pork
Garnished with lime juice and chilli sauce
It is equally delicious without the chilli sauce.

Serves 4

1 lb (450 gm) fresh egg noodles
1 lettuce (finely sliced)
2 tablespoons dark soya sauce
2 to 3 tablespoons vegetable oil
2 medium onions (finely sliced)
1 lb beansprouts (450 gm)

1 or 2 eggs
Use a little chilli sauce if required
1/2 lb (225 gm) bean curd (yellow colour)
   3" x 3" square (cut into thin strips) optional
1/2 lb chicken breast, or lean pork
   (finely sliced) or prawns
For garnish : use a whole lemon (finely sliced)

METHOD:

Wash beansprouts and drain. Heat the wok with oil until quite hot, add the onions and stir fry until light brown. Add the chicken or pork first and stir fry for 5 minutes.
First add the noodles then the soya sauce, bean curd slices, beansprouts and stir until well mixed for about 5 to 6 minutes. If using prawns add prawns after the noodles.
Pour 1 tablespoon of oil into the centre of the wok, crack the eggs in and stir the noodles vigorously.

Use a little chilli sauce if required. When noodles are golden brown in colour, serve on a plate with lettuce and two slices of lemon for garnish.

TIPS:

When using chilli sauce, use only a little drop, if too much is used, it can be very hot.

HOKKIEN MEE (SPICY EGG NOODLE)

This is a very delicious snack, which can be eaten in the morning as breakfast or lunch, or as an evening meal. The egg noodles are boiled separately and then served in a prawn soup, which is very tasty with some chilli sauce garnished with crispy fried onions; perfect served with Chinese leaves, slices of pork and prawns. It is a very popular dish with the Chinese people who love its succulent flavours. A very special favourite of mine when returning home to Penang.

2 lbs prawns (900 gm)
8 oz fresh egg noodles (225 gm)
8 oz Bee Hoon
  (white vermicelli noodles (225 gm)
1 lb bean sprouts (450 gm)
1/2 lb (225 gm) green Chinese leaves
  (cut into 1 inch lengths)
1 lb onions (finely sliced)
1 lb lean pork (finely sliced)
2 to 3 eggs (hard boiled)

1 medium size palm sugar (white sugar
  looks like a piece of transparent rock
  known as "Peng Tung" in Chinese
1/2 teaspoon salt
1 tablespoon sugar (granulated)
3 tablespoons vegetable oil
6 cloves garlic (chopped)
1 dessertspoon soya sauce
1 jar of ready made chilli paste

For garnish: Deep fry the onions until golden brown. Also served with red chilli sauce.

METHOD:

Boil the eggs, peel and put on one side for later. Soak Bee Hoon rice noodles in cold water until soft, about 20 minutes, and drain. Wash prawns with shells on and put into large saucepan to boil for about 30 minutes.

After 15 minutes drain the prawns, peel shells off and mash shells with a heavy metal spoon. Then put shells into a muslin bag, tie with a string and return to the saucepan to continue cooking on medium heat for an hour.

Heat the oil in the wok and stir fry half the chilli paste until light brown, add garlic and stir for 2 minutes, then add sugar, soya sauce and stir until well mixed. Add prawns to the paste and stir again until prawns are dry about 15 minutes. Cool the prawns, make 3 incisions on each prawn with a sharp knife and set aside.

Wash Chinese leaves and beansprouts and drain. Boil both in a separate saucepan for 2 to 3 minutes and leave on one side. Boil the pork for about 20 to 25 minutes until cooked and then drain. Cool first and then finely slice.

Boil Bee Hoon noodle and egg noodle for 2 to 3 minutes in the same saucepan, then dip in cold water and return back into hot water for 1 minute and drain quickly.

Deep fry the onions until golden brown and drain. Take the muslin out of the stock and discard the shells. Drain the stock.

Put egg noodles and rice noodles into 4 individual bowls and decorate with Chinese leaves, beansprouts, a few slices of pork, prawns, egg slices. Pour a little stock over the noodles. Serve with red chilli sauce as a side dish. Garnish with deep fried crispy onions.

PORK FAT

Cut crispy pork fat into small pieces and fry in the wok for about 10 to 15 minutes until oil runny. Use pork oil to stir fry the chilli paste and season with salt to taste. This chilli sauce is used to serve as a side dish. Transfer cold sauce into a pottery or plastic container and seal with a lid. It will keep in a fridge for at least 2 weeks or longer.

Do not use too much chilli sauce or the flavour will be too strong.

(Above) A view of the famous Ayer Itam Temple in Penang. Also on the back cover of this bo

(Above) A meat stall in an indoor market

FRIED BEE HOON - WHITE VERMICELLI NOODLE

Serves 6

1/2 lb (225 gm) frozen prawns
1 medium size onion (sliced)
5 to 6 cloves garlic (chopped)
1/2 lb Chinese leaves cut into 1 inch (2.5 cm) pieces or use 1/2 lb beansprouts instead.
3 tablespoons dark soya sauce
5 tablespoons vegetable oil
1 packet of white vermicelli noodle (soaked in water for 20 minutes until soft and then drain)

METHOD:

Wash the Chinese leaves and cut into 1 inch pieces. Drain the vermicelli noodles until soft and set on one side. Wash the beansprouts and drain.

Heat the oil in wok when hot, add chopped garlic, stirring for 2 to 3 minutes until light brown. Add onions and stir for a further 2 minutes. Next add prawns, continue stirring, then add the noodles and mix well.

Add the dark soya sauce and stir well for 6 to 7 minutes. Add the beansprouts and stir for a further 5 minutes until noodles turn brown.

PENANG LAKSA (ASAM BELAS) HOKKIEN STYLE
WHITE RICE NOODLES IN SPICY FISH SAUCE

Yet another popular snack of Malaya. Both the Chinese and Malay people adore it. It is a white rice noodles which is cooked in a very spicy fish soup, served with mint leaves, cucumber slices and pineapples. It is not very hot, but is very spicy and should be accompanied with a long cold drink.

Serves 4

2 lbs white rice noodles (900 gm)
1 lb tinned sardines or any fish
2 stalks lemon grass (finely sliced)
1 inch (2.5 cm) yellow ginger
15 shallots or use small onions (finely sliced)
1 inch (2.5 cm) blachan (prawn paste)
  cut into small pieces
4 dried or fresh chillies (if using dried chillies
  soak in water until soft and drained)
2 tablespoons tamarind juice (soak a small
  amount of fruit in water for 10 minutes and
  then drained, reserve the juice.

1 pink flower known as "Bunga Kelatan"
  finely chopped if not available, use a few
  curry leaves for substitute, use for aroma.
1 teaspoon sugar
4 pints water (2.25 litres)
1 teaspoon salt
A few slice of pineapple (cut into small
  pieces)
1/2 cucumber (finely sliced and cut into
  thin strips)

For garnish: use a few sprigs of fresh mint leaves, break off the stocks.

METHOD:

First wash the fish if using fresh fish, slit open in the middle and clean. Then cut fish into 2 to 3 pieces. Blend the ginger, onions, blachan (prawn paste) dried chillies and lemon grass into a smooth paste. Use speed 2 to blend, switch off add a little water and stir with a spatula and blend again until smooth.

Boil all the ingredients with the fish in a saucepan with 4 pints of water for 30 minutes. Taste to see if more salt is needed. After boiling put stock through a strainer and reserve just the stock. Discard the rest.

Next boil the rice noodles in another saucepan for 2 to 3 minutes and drain. Put noodles into individual bowls, and pour stock over the noodles. Serve with pineapple pieces, cucumber and garnish with 2 or 3 sprigs of mint leaves.

TIPS:

Tinned sardines can be use instead of fresh ones. Tamarind fruit are sold in packets in Indian or Chinese shops.

CHAR-HOR FUN (STIR FRIED WHITE RICE NOODLES)

Serves 4

2 lb fresh Hor Fun (white rice noodles) 1 inch wide	2 tablespoons water
1\2 lb fresh prawns	1 lb Chinese leaves (cut into 1 inch pieces)
1/2 lb (225 gm) liver (finely sliced)	1 dessertspoon cornflour (mix with a little water to a creamy texture)
1/2 lb (225 gm) lean pork (finely sliced)	6 cloves garlic (chopped)
1 small tin crab meat	1 large onion (finely sliced)
	5 tablespoons vegetable oil

METHOD:

Heat oil in wok until quite hot, add the garlic and onions and stir fry for 2 to 3 minutes until light brown. First add the meat, and stir fry for about 10 minutes.

Then add the noodles and keep stirring for about 3 to 5 minutes, add dark soya sauce and continuing stirring for 5 minutes.

Next add Chinese leaves, stirring for 2 minutes, add 2 tablespoons of water. Finally pour the cornflour mixture into the noodle and stir for about 3 minutes until well mixed. Add a little bit more water if necessary so that it is not too dry. Simmer for 3 minutes and serve.

CURRY MEE
SPICY EGG NOODLES COOKED IN COCONUT MILK

Egg noodles are boiled separately in a saucepan. The soup is cooked with a mixture of curry paste, coconut milk and pork bones. This dish is spicy but not very hot. The egg noodles are served with beancurd slices, beansprouts, cockles and pork slices and is very tasty.

Serves 4

1/2 lb bean curd (cut into small squares)
packet curry paste (already mixed)
cups thick coconut milk plus 4 cups thin coconut milk
lb 450 gm pork bones (boiled for 30 minutes)
1/2 lb lean pork (finely sliced)
lb 900 gm fresh egg noodles
small jar cockles

1/2 lb beansprouts
1/2 teaspoon salt
1 stalk lemon grass (crushed)
1 piece lengkuas about 2 inch piece (crushed) if lengkuas is dried soak in water until soft for about 45 minutes and drained
2 to 3 tablespoons vegetable oil
1 palm sugar (known as "peng tung" in Chinese) about 3 inch piece

METHOD:

Heat wok with oil until hot add the curry paste and stir fry for about 5 minutes until oil separates from paste. Add lemon grass, lengkuas, salt and stir fry for 3 minutes and turn off heat.

Boil pork bones in a deep saucepan for 30 minutes. Then add the fried chilli paste to the stock and stir well. Turn heat down a little and add coconut milk and keep stirring. Add palm sugar and simmer for 20 minutes. Add salt to taste. Boil pork for about 20 minutes or until cooked, when cool, slice finely. Wash beansprouts and boil for 2 to 3 minutes, then drain and set aside.

Boil water in a separate saucepan. When the water has boiled, drop the noodles in for about 2 minutes and then bring them out to drain. Put noodles into individual bowls and pour the spicy stock over them. Serve with beancurd, pork, cockles and beansprouts.

TIPS:

Lengkuas belongs to the ginger family. If fresh Lengkuas are not available, dried ones are sold in Chinese supermarkets and Indian shops.

CHAR KOAY TEOW (STIR FRIED WHITE RICE NOODLES)

1 and 1/4 lb fresh koay teow (white rice noodles about half an inch wide. (561 gm)
1 and 1/2 lb prawns (225 gm)
3 Chinese sausages (finely sliced)
1 lb cooked cockles (450 gm)
4 large eggs

6 cloves garlic (peeled and chopped)
3 to 4 spring onions (cut into 2 inch in lengths)
8 tablespoons vegetable oil
1 lb (450 gm) beansprouts
3 to 4 tablespoons dark soya sauce
1 teaspoon chilli sauce

METHOD:

Wash and drain beansprouts. Break off the brown roots of the bottom of the beansprouts, if you wish. Finely slice the Chinese sausages. Wash the spring onions and cut into 2 inch lengths.

Heat the wok with the oil until quite hot, add the garlic and stir for about 2 minutes until light brown. Then add the prawns and stir for 2 minutes. Add the cockles and the noodles and stir until well mixed. Add the beansprouts and then the soya sauce and continue stirring for 3 minutes. Add Chinese sausages and spring onions and stir again until it is brown in colour.

Put a little oil in the centre of the wok and crack the eggs into the oil and stir in all the noodles until well mixed. Add more soya sauce if necessary to taste. Chilli sauce can be added to the noodles at the end of cooking. Only use a small amount because it is very hot.

TIPS:

Cockles can be bought in any supermarket in jars. Chinese sausages are available in any Chinese supermarket.

MEE JAWA (MALAYAN NOODLE)

Serves 4
1 lb egg noodles (fresh if available, if not use dried noodles)
4 lettuce leaves (finely sliced)
4 pieces yellow colour beancurd 3" x 3" square (sliced into thin strips) after it has been stir fried

1/2 lb lean pork or beef (sliced into thin strips)
3 tablespoons vegetable oil
2 hard boiled eggs
4 medium onions (finely sliced and then deep fried until crispy)
For garnish: use 1 whole lemon (finely sliced)

SAUCE:

2 to 3 tablespoons tomato ketchup
1 teaspoon chilli paste - (also known as "sambal" in Malay)
A pinch of aji - no - moto
A pinch of pepper
1 clove garlic (chopped)

Sweet corn and Crab soup (above)
Mee Goreng stir fried noodle (bottom)

METHOD:

Wash lettuce finely slice then drain. Mix sauce ingredients together in a blender and blend into a smooth mixture. Then put the sauce into a saucepan and beat until creamy on low heat, stirring constantly.

Boil the eggs for about 10 minutes then put into cold water to cool and peel off the shells and slice. Set on one side. Heat two tablespoons of oil in the wok until it is quite hot, add the pork or beef and stir fry over medium heat for about 10 to 15 minutes until cooked. Use another frying pan, heat 1 tablespoon of oil, and stir fry the bean curd 2 minutes each side and then slice them into thin strips

If using dried noodles boil the egg noodles in a separate saucepan in hot boiling water, then drain. If using fresh noodles dip the noodles in the hot boiling water for 1 to 2 minutes and drained. Put into 4 individual bowls.

Put slices of pork or beef on top of the noodles, add lettuce leaves, slices bean curds, lemon wedges for garnish. Pour hot sauce over the noodles and sprinkle with crispy fried onions.

BAK POW (STEAMED DUMPLINGS) DIM SUM

Steamed dumplings are made from three different flavours and fillings:

1   Chicken, mushrooms and egg
2   Roast pork fillings
3   Coconut jam

It is served for breakfast in a tea house.

Dumplings can be microwaved. Use 850 Watt power. Place a plate of hot water in the microwave and then put the wet bamboo steamer on top of the plate and place the dumplings inside the bamboo container and cover with the lid and steam for about 20 minutes.

Makes 9 individual servings.

FILLINGS:

1/2 tablespoons dark soya sauce	3 teaspoons sugar
1/2 lb lean pork (sliced)	A pinch of salt
8 eggs	A pinch of pepper
1/4 lb martai(water chestnuts) optional	1 teaspoon dried ginger or crushed fresh ginger
1 tablespoon corn flour	8 oz Chinese mushrooms (soaked in water
1 tablespoon corn oil or lard	until soft then drained and sliced)
1 teaspoon sesame oil	1 large onion (peeled and sliced)
1 teaspoon salt	

Dim Sum (Steamed Dumplings)

DOUGH:

1/2 lb wheat flour	5 tablespoons water
3 teaspoons baking powder	1 tablespoon lard
6 tablespoons sugar	

METHOD:

Mix flour, water baking powder, sugar, lard and knead the flour in a bowl. Let it stand for half an hour until risen.
Whilst waiting, heat the sesame oil in the wok and stir fry the onions until light brown for 2 to 3 minutes.

Add meat slices and mushrooms and stir fry for 6 to 8 minutes. If using chestnuts, peel and chop chestnuts and add to the meat and stir, add salt, sugar, pepper ginger.

Mix cornflour with a little water to a smooth cream and add to the mixture. Stir it well for about 10 minutes. Add soya sauce and stir again for 3 minutes.
Boil the eggs until hard-boiled. Peel egg shells and slice eggs into 4 quarters and add to the meat. Add 1 cup of water (1/4 pint) and boil for about 10 minutes until meat is cooked.
Put on one side to cool. Use for fillings.
Knead the dough. Take 2 inches of the dough and roll into a ball, then roll it flat with a rolling pin. Use one dessertspoon of fillings, gather pastry into the centre and seal it with cornflour.

Place dumplings on 3" x 3" grease proof paper and steam for about 5 minutes until well risen.

MALAYAN SATAY

This is one of Malaysian's favourite dish. Satays are made from meat either from chicken, beef, prawns or lamb. The meat is cut into small pieces and marinated in a dish overnight or for at least 2 to 3 hours before grilling. The meat pieces are put onto a metal skewer about 5 inches long, making sure there is enough space to hold the skewer. In Malaya satays are grilled over an open fire with wooden sticks. Soak bamboo sticks for half an hour until soft to avoid breaking. Satays are served with peanut sauce, rice, sliced cucumbers and onions as a side dish.

Makes 6 to 7 sticks

1 lb lean beef or chicken or lamb (450 gm) cut into thin strips.	1 teaspoon salt
1 stalk lemon grass fresh (finely sliced) or use 1 tablespoons dried.	2 inch (5 cm) saffron or use 1/2 teaspoon turmeric
2 inch (5 cm) fresh ginger (finely sliced)	1 inch (2.5 cm) lengkuas, vegetable looks like ginger finely sliced (optional)
2 teaspoons aniseed powder (jintan manis)	
2 teaspoons cummin seeds (jintan puteh)	2 tablespoons sugar
2 tablespoons coriander powder (ketumbah)	2 tablespoons vegetable oil

Malayan Satay with Peanut sauce

METHOD:

Heat the saucepan with oil until quite hot. Mix cummin seeds, aniseeds, coriander and stir fry until light brown for 2 to 3 minutes and set aside.

Blend lemon grass, ginger. saffron, lengkuas into a smooth paste. Switch off blender and stir with a spatula. Add a little water if necessary.

Cut meat into fine strips and mix with salt, sugar and then paste together to marinate and leave it in a pyrex for about 2 hours.

After that mix all the other spice ingredients together. Put meat onto a skewer and grill for about 2 to 3 minutes each side until brown in colour. While grilling baste with marinade sauce.

TIPS:

If using fresh lemon grass, only use 6 inches from the bottom onwards and discard the rest. Lemon grass is also known as "serai" in Malay. Use double the meat amount if you need more sticks.

SATAY SAUCE

1 lb (450 gm) peanuts
6 fresh red chillies or use 3 if you prefer
  it mild or use dried chillies instead.
1 to 2 stalks lemon grass (chopped)
  use 6 inches from the bottom onwards
2 inches lengkuas or use half the amount,
  soak in water until soft, drained and
  finely slice

6 shallots or onions equivalent or use half
  the amount (peeled and sliced)
1/2 inch fresh ginger (finely sliced)
2 inch piece tamarind fruit (soak fruit in
  water for 15 minutes and drained, reserve
  the juice about half a cup.
2 tablespoons vegetable oil
2 tablespoons of sugar

METHOD:

Put peanuts into a grinder for 3 to 5 minutes.
Pound or blend all the ingredients that is chillies, lemon grass, lengkuas, shallots and ginger into a smooth paste. Add a little water if necessary. Switch off and stir with a spatula.
Heat the saucepan with the oil until quite hot, add the paste and stir fry for 5 to 6 minutes until brown. Next add ground peanuts, sugar, salt, and sufficient tamarind juice to taste. Stir over a low heat for about 8-10 minutes until creamy.
The sauce is now ready to serve with the meat satay, use for dipping. It is also served with a plate of sliced cucumbers and cubed onions as a side dish.

TIPS:

Lengkuas is also known as "galangal" or "Laos Powder". Lengkuas is sold in dried packet already sliced. Soak in water until soft and drained before use.

If using dried chillies, soak chillies in water for about 20 minutes until very soft and then drain.

STEAM - BOAT PENANG STYLE

A traditional style of entertaining. This dish is enjoyed at home on special occasions including Chinese New Year's Eve. Steamed boat is a name for a very special dish. A variety of vegetables and meat are used and arranged on separate trays. The steamer is placed on a charcoal burner in the centre of the table and filled with meat stock. The vegetables are dropped into the stock for 2 to 3 minutes and then drained and put onto a plate.

Served with: Plain rice, chilli sauce or a small bowl of soup

Serves six to eight persons
2 pints Chicken or Pork Stock
1 teaspoon of Aji-no-moto
1/2 teaspoon of Salt

Method:

Put all ingredients together and bring to the boil in a saucepan for 25 to 30 mins. Then transfer into Steam-boat container. This container has a charcoal burner.

6 to 8 eggs	1 lb. Fish balls (round white ball)
1 lb. lean Pork (sliced - not too thin)	1 lb. Fish fillets (cut into 1 inch size slices)
1 lb. King Prawns (peel prawns, omitting the tails)	1 lb. Beef (sliced)
1 lb. Chinese Cabbage - cut into 2 inches long.	

Method:

Wash the prawns. Cut the cabbage and slice the beef and pork. Wash fish slit and clean. Arrange the meat and vegetables on separate plates and put the steamboat in the centre of the table. When stock is boiling each person drops in the meat and vegetables for 1/2 mins. and then lift them out and put on their plates. It's a help yourself thing. Tomato and chilli sauce are put into a small plates as a side dishes. Fresh red chillies are sliced into a dish sprinkled with soya sauce. Pickled green chillies go down very well too.

KRABU VEGETABLE SALAD (MALAYAN)

1 onion (finely sliced)
1 medium cabbage (finely sliced)
1 inch fresh ginger root (finely sliced)
1/2 lb bean sprouts (225 gm)
2 tablespoons tamarind juice (juice from
  tamarind fruit, soak fruit in a small bowl
  for about 10 minutes and save the juice.
  Discard the stones.

1 red fresh chilli (finely sliced)
2 tomatoes (sliced)
1 inch piece blachan 2.5 cm (prawn paste
  cut into small pieces)
4 oz roasted grated coconut

METHOD:

Put the chilli, tomatoes, prawn paste into an electric blender and blend until smooth. Add a little water if necessary to help it blend properly.

Mix onions, cabbage, ginger root, bean sprouts together in a large bowl and add grated coconut. Stir it well and pour tamarind juice over the salad.

Mix the chilli paste with the salad. This is used as a side dish to go with curry dishes. It can be eaten with plain rice.

TIPS:

Tamarind fruit has a sweet and sour taste.

STIR FRIED CHINESE CABBAGE

1 Ib (450 gm) Chinese cabbage or
  use spinach
1/2 lb (225 gm) prawns
1 large carrot (finely sliced or grated)
5 cloves of garlic (chopped)
2 tablespoons vegetable oil

2 to 3 tablespoons water
1/2 teaspoon Aji - no - moto (Gourmet
  Powder)
1 dessertspoon cornflour (mix with a
  little water to a creamy mixture)
1 tablespoon oyster sauce

METHOD:

Wash the cabbage or spinach and slice into 1 inch pieces. Heat the oil in wok until add garlic and stir fry until light brown.

Add prawns and stir fry for 3 to 4 minutes then add carrots and Chinese cabbage. Add oyster sauce and water and stir until creamy. Turn heat down a little before adding cornflour mixture and aji - no - moto and salt to taste. Simmer for 6 to 8 minutes until meat is tender.

Stir fried Green Beans with Prawns (top) Beancurd Soup (bottom)

STIR FRIED MIXED VEGETABLES

1/2 lb lean pork (finely sliced) 225 gm
5 cloves garlic (chopped)
1/4 Ib brown bean curd (112 gm) small
  squares shaped
1/3 oz Tang-Hoon (very fine transparent
  rice noodles)
25 gm 1 small cauliflower (cut into bite
  size pieces)
1 large carrot (finely sliced or grated)

1 tablespoon oyster sauce
1/4 oz dried Chinese mushrooms (soaked in
  water until soft and drained)
2 to 3 tablespoons water
1/4 teaspoon aji - no - moto (Gourmet
  Powder)
1/4 teaspoon salt
2 tablespoons vegetable oil
1 dessertspoon cornflour (mix with a little
  water until creamy)

METHOD:

Wash pork, pat dry and finely slice. Soak rice noodles in cold water for 5 to 10 minutes until soft and drained. When mushrooms are soft, drain and then slice them.

Heat the oil until hot add garlic and stir fry until light brown. Add pork and stir for 5 to 6 minutes, then add cauliflower, carrots, mushrooms and stir fry for a further 5 minutes. Add rice noodles and stir until well mix.

Then add bean curd with 2 to 3 tablespoons of water and aji - no - moto and salt. Add oyster sauce and turn heat down a little before adding cornflour mixture to the vegetables and simmer for 5 to 6 minutes and simmer for 6 to 8 minutes.

SPICY OKRA (INDIAN STYLE)

1 lb fresh okras or also known as "ladies
  fingers" (a green long vegetable shaped
  like a finger)
1 large onion (peeled and finely sliced)
3 tablespoons vegetable oil
1 tablespoon salt

1/2 teaspoon coriander powder
1/2 teaspoon cummin seeds
1/2 teaspoon red chilli powder
1/8 teaspoon turmeric powder
1 small tin plum tomato
A pinch of pepper

METHOD:

First wash okras, drain and slice it diagonally. Heat two tablespoons oil in the wok and stir fry the okras on a medium heat for about 10 minutes until nearly soft.

Heat another pan with 1 tablespoon of oil and when it is quite hot, add the onions and stir fry until golden brown. Add the coriander, cummin seeds, turmeric, pepper and stir for 5 minutes.

Then add the tomato and stir fry slowly for about 10 minutes. Next add the okras to the spicy onion sauce. Add chilli powder and salt and then reduce the heat and simmer for 5 minutes.

Chicken with mushroom and baby corns in Oyster Sauce

MIXED VEGETABLE CURRY (INDIAN STYLE)

3 Medium onions (finely sliced)
1/4 teaspoon turmeric
2 tablespoons vegetable oil
1 teaspoon coriander powder
1 clove garlic (peeled and sliced)
1 small tin tomato
1 inch (2.5 cm) fresh ginger (finely sliced)
1/2 teaspoon cummin seeds
1 small jar natural yoghurt
2 inch piece cinnamon stick

2 or 3 green chillies (finely sliced)
4 oz green beans or peas
1 teaspoon salt
1 small cauliflower (cut into small pieces)
2 medium size carrots (peeled and finely sliced)
1 small cabbage (finely sliced)
1/2 teaspoon red chilli powder
1 and a half cup of water
For garnish: use a few sprigs of fresh coriander leaves (chopped)

METHOD:

Wash all the vegetables and slice them. Heat a deep saucepan with oil until quite hot and add the onions, stir fry until golden brown. Add the ginger and garlic and stir for 2 minutes. Then add the ground coriander and cummin seeds and stir again. After 3 minutes add salt, red chilli powder, turmeric, tomatoes and green chillies.
Stir fry for 5 minutes, turn heat down low and add 2 to 3 tablespoons of yoghurt and stir for 10 minutes. Finally add all the vegetables and one and a half cups of water and boil for 10 minutes. During cooking add fresh coriander leaves for garnish. Use more salt if required.

SIMPLE SALAD DISH

1 medium size onion (finely sliced)
1/2 cucumber (finely sliced)
2 or 3 green chillies (finely sliced)

SAUCE:

1 or 2 tablespoons white vinegar
1/2 pint water
1 dessertspoon sugar

METHOD:

Wash cucumber and cut into halves lengthways and then finely slice diagonally. Wash chillies and finely slice.

Use a small saucepan to boil the vinegar, water and sugar together for about 5 minutes. Switch off cooker.

Put all the vegetables in a large serving bowl and pour the hot sauce over the vegetables. This is used as a side dish.

PICKLED MIXED VEGETABLES AH CHAT AH WAT

Fresh raw vegetables are used for this dish. You can use less chillies about 3 to 4 if you prefer it mild. It is served as a side dish with for example, beancurds cooked with prawns and spring onions. It tastes very spicy but not hot.

10 small shallots (peeled)

2 stalks lemon grass (finely sliced) also known as "serai" in Malaya

2 cloves garlic (peeled)

2 inch piece prawn paste known as "blachan" in Malaya cut into small pieces

5 dried chillies (soaked in water until soft and drained)

2 dessertspoons sugar

1 inch piece (2.5 cm) yellow ginger (finely sliced)

2 tablespoons vegetable oil 6 candlenuts also known as "buah keras" in Malaya

4 oz ground nuts (eg. peanuts) already pecled

1 small tin pineapple chunks

1 medium size cucumber (cut into half lengthways then finely sliced diagonally)

1 small cabbage (finely sliced) or 1/2 lb greens or french beans (finely sliced)

1/4 pint of vinegar

METHOD:

Wash and slice vegetables. Blend the shallots, lemon grass, garlic, chillies, ginger, candle nuts and prawn paste into a smooth paste. Add a little water if necessary. Switch off and stir with a spatula.

Heat 2 tablespoons of oil in a large saucepan when quite hot, add the paste and stir fry until brown for 3 to 4 minutes.

Add the vinegar to the paste and stir again for a further 1 minute.

Next add the vegetables and stir fry until well mix for about 5 to 6 minutes. Then add pineapple, salt and sugar and keep stirring. Turn heat down a little and add ground nuts. Continue stirring and simmer about 10 minutes on medium heat. Do not add any water to vegetables. Turn off heat and cool the vegetables. Once it has been cooled it can be stored in jars and kept in fridge for upto 1 to 2 weeks.

SWEET AND SOUR VEGETABLES

1 small green pepper (deseeded and cut into small pieces)

1 medium carrot

1 small white cabbage (cut into small squares) about 1 inch

1 small onion (cut into 1 inch pieces)

1/2 cucumber (cut into half lengthways then sliced diagonally)

1/2 lb mushrooms (peeled and finely sliced)

1 small tin pineapple chunks

1 dessertspoon cornflour (mixed with a little water to a creamy mixture)

2 tablespoons tomato ketchup

2 to 3 tablespoons vegetable oil

1 tablespoon vinegar

1 dessertspoon sugar

A man selling
"Koay Kak" stir
fried steamed rice

METHOD:

First mix cornflour wih a little water to a creamy mixture and set on one side. Wash cabbage and cut into small squares. Wash and deseed pepper and cut into small pieces. Peel and finely slice the carrot diagonally. Cut cucumber into half lengthways and then finely slice diagonally.

Heat oil in wok until quite hot on medium heat, add onions and stir fry until light brown for about 2 minutes. Add cabbage and carrot and stir for 2 to 3 minutes. Then add pepper, cucumber, pineapple and mushrooms and keep stirring for about 5 minutes.

Next add pineapple juice, tomato ketchup and vinegar and stir until well mixed. Turn heat down a little and add the cornflour mixture. Add sugar to taste and stir simmer for about 10 minutes until vegetables are soft. Add more water if necessary so that sauce is not too thick.

TOW - FU WITH PRAWNS (BEAN CURD WITH PRAWNS)

or 2 piece of tow -fu (white bean curds)
squares
tablespoons of vegetable oil
cup of water
clove garlic (chopped)
/2 lb prawns (peeled)

1 dessertspoon oyster sauce
A pinch of salt
1 dessertspoon light soya sauce
2 oz of chye poh (pickled beans already
  chopped)

METHOD:

Cut tow -fu (bean curds) into several pieces. Wash and peel prawns. Heat oil in wok until quite hot, fry the garlic until brown for 1 min. then add prawns, and stir for 1 or 2 mins. Add tow - fu, oyster sauce, light soya sauce, salt and water.

Add aji - no - moto and boil for about 6 to 8 mins. add chopped spring onions for garnish.

HOW TO MAKE BEAN CURD (TOW -FU)

Makes 275 gm (Tow-Fu) 10 oz
Makes 275 gm (Okara) or Soya Bran 10 oz

200 gm Soya beans
Juice of 2 lemons

METHOD:

Put beans in a bowl cover with water overnight in a cool place. Do not leave in warm place or it will ferment. Drain and rinse thoroughly. Liquidize beans to a creamy consistency, using one cup of water for each cup of beans. This is called "GO".

Bring 6 cups of water to the boil in a large saucepan. When boiling add the liquidized soya beans. Bring back to the boil. When the mixture boils up to the top of the pan, sprinkle cold water over it. This will stop the boiling and the liquid will sink back.

Repeat this 3 times stirring occasionally. This stage is very important as it destroys any toxins in the bean skin. Line a colander with muslin and place over a clean bowl. Strain the mixture into it. The crumbly residue in the muslin is called "OKARA" OR "SOYA BRAN". The liquid is soya milk.

Return the soya milk to a clean saucepan and bring to the boil. Pour into a clean bowl. Add the juice of 2 lemons. Stir very gently then leave the mixture to curdle, if it doesn't bring the liquid back to the boil and add more lemon juice.

Using a fine sieve, press lightly against the curds in the bowl and scoop out the liquid with a ladle. Very gently tip the curds into a colander lined with muslin. Allow the moisture to drain off. This is soft or silken Tow - Fu.

For a firmer Tow - fu, wrap the curds in muslin and weigh them down. The heavier the weight and the longer it is left, the more solid the Tow - Fu will be.

TIPS:

It will keep for a week in the refridgerator.
It can be frozen in a plastic container.

BEAN-CURD FRITTERS (TOW-KWAH)

4 yellow beancurd squares 3" x 3"
1/2 lb minced pork (225 gm)
A pinch of salt
A pinch of Aji - no - moto

1 large egg
1 litre of vegetable oil for deep-frying
A pinch of pepper

METHOD:

Cut the beancurd into halves diagonally so it looks like a triangle. Slit the middle with a sharp knife ready for filling and set on one side.

Put minced pork into a bowl, add salt, pepper, and aji - no - moto. Then crack an egg into the centre of the bowl and mix with a fork until quite thick.

Use 1 dessertspoonful of meat to fill into the middle of the beancurd. Then deep-fry the beancurd in wok until brown for 2 minutes on each side. Drain the beancurd on kitchen paper on a plate to absorb the oil. Serve with cucumber slices, onion rings and chilli or tomato sauce.

(Above) A Chinese man selling all kinds of vegetables in a market

(Above) A view of the indoor market, showing fish stall

BEEF WITH PINEAPPLE

8 oz beef (225 gm)
1 small tin of pineapple (sliced)
1 clove of garlic (chopped)

A pinch of ground black pepper
2 tablespoons vegetable oil
A pinch of salt

METHOD:

Cut beef into bite pieces, mix beef with small amount of oil, salt, and pepper and leave for 5 mins. Heat the wok with oil until it is quite hot, add garlic and fry for 3 mins. then add beef. Stir fry for about 10 mins. over medium heat, add pineapple and stir for another 5 mins. Finally add sauce.

HOW TO MAKE SAUCE:

2 teaspoons of cornflour, 2 tablespoons oyster sauce, 2 tablespoons water.

Put oyster sauce in a small saucepan over low heat, mix cornflour with water to a creamy texture. Add to the sauce, keep stirring add water, as soon as it bubbles turn off heat. Add sauce to the beef and pineapple and stir well. Transfer it into a serving dish.

INDIAN BEEF CURRY

1 lb beef (sliced into thin strips)
1 large onion (peeled and finely sliced)
4 oz of peas (optional) boil for 2 to 3
  minutes and drained
6 cloves of garlic (peeled and chopped)
1/4 teaspoon red chilli powder
3 tablespoons vegetable oil

1 and 1/2 teaspoon salt
3 cups of water
1/2 teaspoon masala
2 or 3 green chillies (finely sliced)
For garnish: use a few sprigs of fresh
  coriander leaves (chopped)

METHOD:

Put beef with other ingredients except garam masala and peas into a pressure cooker with 1 cup of water and steam for about 7 to 8 minutes. Switch off cooker and let off steam and open the lid.
Test to see if the meat is soft, by pricking with a fork. If there is still water in the pressure cooker continue cooking without the lid until water is nearly dry.

When the saucepan is nearly dry, add 3 tablespoons oil to the beef. Add garam masala and peas and stir fry on medium heat for about 10 minutes until meat is brown.

Add two cups of water and boil for 5 minutes then turn heat down and simmer for 5 minutes. During cooking add chopped coriander leaves. Taste to see if you need more salt.

If using 2 lbs of beef use half a teaspoon of red chilli powder. If using 3 lbs of beef use 1 teaspoon of red chilli powder.

INDIAN LAMB CURRY

1 teaspoon garam masala
1 - 2 lbs onion (sliced)
2 lbs lamb fillet (or chicken pieces)
2 tablespoons vegetable oil
2 - 3 green chillies (whole crushed)

1 piece root ginger 2.5cm (finely sliced)
1 - 2 dessertspoons tomato puree
2 fresh tomatoes (chopped)
1/2 teaspoon salt
1/2 pint water

METHOD:

Wash and cut lamb into bite size pieces. Wash tomatoes and chop into small pieces. Wash and crush green chillies and put one aside for garnish later.
Heat a large saucepan with oil until quite hot, add all the onions and give it a good stir until golden brown for 1 to 2 minutes.

Next add garam masala and then add crushed chillies and stir again for 1 to 2 minutes. Add root ginger and mix well.

Now add the lamb pieces and stir frequently for a few minutes. Let it simmer for about 30 minutes over moderate heat until lamb is tender.
Add tomato puree 1 to 2 dessertspoons and chopped tomatoes and let it boil for 3 minutes, add more water if necessary and salt to taste.
Serve with boiled rice

TIPS:

Chicken can be used instead of lamb. If using chicken let it cook for an extra 1/4 an hour.

SPICY CHILLI CRABS

This is a crab dish normally eaten with rice. It is a very delicious, mouth watering dish, cooked in a spicy chilli sauce with brown salted beans and candle nuts.

Before cooking the crab it should be cut into pieces:
A medium sized crab should be cut into half
A large crab should be cut into 4 quarters

Once cooked the crab is placed on a plate and a hammer used to break the claws open in order to extract the maximum amount of meat.

Once tasted you will be asking for more.

3 lbs medium crabs or king crabs
6 dried chillies (soaked in water until soft
   and drained)
1 inch (2.5 cm) blachan (prawn paste)
10 shallots or small onions (sliced)
1 clove garlic (chopped)
Buah Keras is known as (candle nuts or cashew nuts)

1 small tin of salted beans (brown colour)
2 large eggs
1/4 cup of water
5 tablespoons of vegetable oil

METHOD:

Wash crabs first, then chop them into halves. Pound or blend chillies, prawn paste, shallots, garlic, and candle nuts together into a smooth paste. Switch off blender and stir with a spatula.

Heat oil in wok until quite hot, add the paste and fry for 3 mins until light brown. Add crabs to the chilli paste. Stir well for 10 minutes add salted brown beans to the crabs mixture. Add 1/2 pint of water and salt to taste. Cover the wok with a lid for about 8 minutes but do not allow it to get dry. Add more water if necessary. Crack 2 eggs into the crabs mixture and continue stirring. The crabs should be pink in colour when cooked.

INDIAN CHICKEN CURRY

3 lb chicken (cut into joints) or use chicken
   drumsticks
2 medium onions (finely sliced)
2 to 3 tablespoons vegetable oil
1 clove garlic (chopped)
1 large tin tomato
1 inch 2.5cm piece fresh ginger (finely sliced)
1/2 teaspoon cummin seeds
1 inch piece cinnamon stick
1/2 teaspoon turmeric powder

1 dessertspoon sugar
1 teaspoon salt
2 or 3 green chillies (finely sliced)
1 teaspoon corriander powder
1/2 pint of water
2 to 3 tablespoons natural yoghurt
1/2 teaspoon red chilli powder
For garnish: use a few sprigs of fresh coriander leaves (chopped)

METHOD:

Wash and cut chicken into joints. Peel and finely slice the onions. Peel and chop the garlic and ginger. Wash the green chillies and finely slice. Chop the corriander leaves and set aside for garnish.
Heat the oil in a large deep saucepan on medium heat until quite hot, add the onions and stir fry until light brown. Add ginger and garlic and stir for 2 to 3 minutes.

After stirring for 3 minutes, add corriander powder, cummin seeds, chilli powder, turmeric and cinnamon stick. Stir until well mixed for 5 minutes.

Add salt, tomato and stir frequently for a further 2 to 3 minutes. Turn heat down a little, add yoghurt and continue stirring for 1 minute.

Add chicken pieces and stir again for about 10 minutes, add water and stir again. Boil for about 10 to 15 minutes during cooking, add chopped corriander and green chillies.

Simmer for about 30 minutes until chicken is tender.

CHICKEN WITH PEPPER IN BLACK BEAN SAUCE

lb chicken breast 450 gm (remove skin from breast)
green pepper (cut into 1 inch squares)
medium onion (finely sliced)
to 5 cloves garlic (chopped)

2 tablespoons vegetable oil
2 tablespoons black bean sauce
4 to 5 tablespoons water

METHOD:

First of all wash and deseed the pepper and cut into small squares. Wash chicken, pat dry and cut into joints. Heat the wok with oil over medium heat. When it gets hot add garlic and stir fry for 1 minute until light brown.

Add the onions and stir for 1 minute, then add the chicken pieces and stir well for 5 to 6 minutes. Add green peppers and stir again for 2 to 3 minutes. Next add black bean sauce and 4 to 5 tablespoons of water and stir well.

Cover with lid and simmer for 10 to 15 minutes on medium heat until chicken is tender. Add more water if necessary so that it won't get too dry. Serve with boiled or fried rice.

FRIED CHICKEN WITH SPRING ONIONS

Serves 4
piece chicken portions
spring onions (sliced diagonally)
medium size onion (peeled and finely sliced)
tablespoons oyster sauce

3 tablespoons vegetable oil
1 dessertspoon cornflour (mix with a little water to a creamy mixture)
A pinch of salt

METHOD:

Wash chicken and pat dry with paper towel. Heat wok with 2 tablespoons of oil until hot enough add the onions and stir fry until brown. Add chicken pieces and stir fry for about 10 to 15 minutes on medium heat and then set aside.

Heat another frying pan with 1 tablespoon oil until hot, add spring onions and stir fry for about 2 minutes. Add oyster sauce and then turn heat down before adding the cornflour mixture. Add salt to taste and stir until it bubbles and pour it over the chicken pieces. Add a little water if necessary so that sauce is not too thick.

CHINESE CHICKEN CURRY

3 lb chicken (450 gm) cut into bite size pieces
6 dried chillies (soaked in water until soft,
  then drained)
2 stalks lemon grass (sliced finely)
1 inch piece 2.5 cm yellow ginger (sliced)
5 cloves garlic (peeled and chopped)

1/2 lb small potatoes (peeled)
1 inch piece 2.5 cm blachan (prawn paste)
  cut into small pieces
1 1/2 pints coconut milk
4 tablespoons vegetable oil
3 tablespoons coriander powder

METHOD:

Wash chicken and cut into bite size pieces. Blend the ingredients, that is lemon grass, yellow ginger, garlic, shallots and blachan (prawn paste) into smooth paste. Stir it with a spatula. Add half of the coriander powder to this mixture and mix well. Heat the wok and use 4 tablespoons of vegetable oil to fry the paste until brown stirring all the time over medium heat.
Mix some of the coriander powder with a small amount of water and stir into the paste mixture. Add the chicken pieces and potatoes stirring frequently for 10 mins. If dry add more water and add salt to taste. Finally add coconut milk to cover the chicken completely over medium heat. Boil for 20 to 25 mins until chicken is tender.

TIPS:

If fresh coconut milk is not available use 2 tablespoons dried coconut milk. If bunga kelatan is not available use 6 curry leaves instead.

MALAYAN CHICKEN CURRY

This traditional chicken curry is always a favourite of both the Chinese and Malay people. The Malayan people like to cook the chicken with lemon grass which is chopped finely to give a nice flavour to the curry. It has a very spicy taste and it is delicious with plain rice. Potatoes can be added to the curry instead of mixed vegetables.

3 lb chicken (450 gm) or use chicken breast
  or drumsticks
2 to 3 tablespoons peanut or vegetable oil
1 medium size onion (peeled and sliced)
1/2 inch piece ginger (finely sliced)
3 cloves garlic (chopped)
1 to 2 stalks lemon grass (chopped finely)
1 dessertspoon ground coriander

2 teaspoons turmeric powder
1/2 teaspoon cayenne pepper
1 cup water
1 dessertspoon tomato paste
1 teaspoon salt
1/2 cup thick coconut milk (dried packet of
  coconut milk is sold in Chinese
Supermarket)
2 to 3 star-anise

Malayan Chicken Curry

METHOD:

Wash chicken, pat dry with paper towel and cut into joints. Use an electric blender to blend the onion, ginger, garlic and lemon grass into a smooth paste for about 3 minutes. Add a little water if necessary so that it is not too thick. Switch off and stir with a spatula.

Heat the saucepan with oil until quite hot, add star-anise and stir fry for about 20 seconds over medium heat, then add the paste and stir again for a further 3 minutes. Add the dry spices to the paste. Stir frequently for another 3 minutes until oil separates from paste.

Next turn heat down add water, salt, tomato paste and coconut milk and boil over low heat for about 5 minutes. Add chicken pieces and continue stirring. Simmer for about 30 minutes until chicken is tender. Add more salt if necessary. Served with boiled rice.

TIPS:

For thick coconut milk mix with 100 ml water. For thinner coconut milk mix with 200 ml water.

CHICKEN IN OYSTER SAUCE

3 lb chicken or 4 chicken breasts
 or 6 chicken drumsticks
2 oz dried Chinese mushrooms (soaked
 in water until soft then drained and sliced)
3 cloves garlic (chopped)
1 to 2 tablespoons oyster sauce
2 oz dried seaweed (soaked in water until
 soft, then drained)

1 dessertspoon sugar
1 inch piece fresh ginger (2.5 cm) finely
 sliced
3 tablespoons vegetable oil
1 dessertspoon cornflour (mix with a little
 water to a creamy mixture)
1 cup of water

METHOD:

Wash chicken and pat dry with paper towel and cut into joints. Heat wok with the oil until quite hot add garlic and stir fry until light brown.

First add ginger and stir fry for 1 minute, then add chicken pieces stirring continously for about 10 to 15 minutes. Next add seaweed, oyster sauce and sugar.

Then turn heat down add cornflour mixture and stir into the chicken for a further 3 minutes. Add the water and let it boil for about 5 minutes and simmer for 10 to 15 minutes until chicken is tender. Add more water if necessary.

SESAME CHICKEN

10 ounce chicken breast (remove skin from chicken)
5 pieces of white bread
3 ounce white sesame seeds (75 gm)

SEASONING:

1 teaspoon salt
1 teaspoon cornflour
1 tablespoon egg white

1/4 teaspoon sesame oil
A pinch of pepper
1 litre of vegetable oil for deep- frying

METHOD:

Clean and pat dry chicken breast with a paper towel. Cut into 1 inch cubes and put meat into mincer. Then switch off and empty chicken meat into a bowl and mix with all the seasonings including the egg white.
Wash and drain the sesame seeds and mix together with the chicken. Cut bread into 2 inch pieces and spread chicken meat onto the bread.

Heat the wok with a litre of oil until very hot and drop the bread in the hot oil and stir fry 2 minutes each side until golden brown. After it is golden brown take the bread out and put onto the kitchen paper to absorb the oil. Serve with a side dish of salad.

CHICKEN IN SPICY GINGER SAUCE

1 whole chicken 3 lb (cut into bite size
  pieces or use 4 chicken breasts
1 inch piece fresh yellow ginger (finely
  sliced) or use 1/2 teaspoon turmeric powder
1/2 dessertspoon curry powder
4 or 5 shallots (peeled and sliced)
4 or 5 cloves garlic (peeled and sliced)

1 or 2 stalks of lemon grass (also known as
  "serai" in Malay) finely sliced
1/2 dessertspoon red chilli powder or use
  half the amount if you prefer it mild
2 to 3 tablespoons vegetable oil
A pinch of salt
1 cup of water
1 dessertspoon sugar

METHOD:

Wash chicken and cut into bite size pieces. Blend the shallots, lemon grass and garlic into a smooth paste. Add a little water if necessary. Switch off blender and stir the paste with a spatula.
Heat the oil in the wok until quite hot, stir fry the paste until brown on medium heat. Add the curry powder and stir for a few minutes. Then add the chicken pieces to the paste and mix well, keep stirring for 5 to 6 minutes.
Add turmeric powder and enough water to cover the chicken. Add salt and some sugar to taste. Simmer for 15 to 20 minutes until chicken is tender.

TIPS:

If fresh lemon grass is not available, use 1 tablespoon dried lemon grass, soaked in water until soft and drained. For fresh lemon grass, only use 6 inches from the bottom upwards.

CHICKEN IN GINGER SAUCE

3 lb chicken (cut into bite size pieces)
1/2 tablespoon Tow - Cheon (brown beans)
  in tin or jar

1 glass of water
2 tablespoons vegetable oil
1" piece ginger 2.5 cm (finely sliced)

METHOD:

Heat wok with oil and fry the chicken pieces for about 8 to 10 mins. Stir well and add 1/2 tablespoon brown beans and a glass of water. Stir again for a further 1 min. and add the ginger and cover wok with a lid and simmer for another 10 mins until chicken is cooked.

TIPS:

Tow Cheon (brown beans) is available in any Chinese shop.

SWEET AND SOUR DUCK

1 duck (450 gm) cut into joints
1 large onion (peeled and cut into small squares)
1 small tin pineapple (sliced and drained sliced)
1/4 cucumber (sliced diagonally)
2 tablespoons tomato sauce
2 tablespoons vinegar
3 tablespoons pineapple juice
1 dessertspoon cornflour (mix with a little water to creamy mixture)

3 pineapple rings use for decoration
2 oz baby pea pods
2 to 3 tablespoons vegetable oil
A pinch of salt
A pinch of black pepper
1 dessertspoon sugar
3 tablespoons water

METHODS:

First mix cornflour with a little water add tomato sauce and vinegar to a creamy mixture and set aside. Wash and clean duck and cut into joints. Peel and cut onions into small squares. Wash cucumber, cut into half lengthways, then finely sliced diagonally. Wash pea pods.
Heat oil in wok until quite hot, add the onions and stir fry until brown for about 3 minutes. Add the duck and stir for a further 8 to 10 minutes on medium heat.

Add pea pods and stir fry for about 2 to 3 minutes then add cucumber, pineapples and stir until well mixed.

Add pineapple juice to the duck, then turn heat down a little. Add cornflour mixture and simmer for about 10 to 15 minutes until meat is tender. Add sugar, salt and pepper to taste.

Add more water if necessary so that the sauce is not too thick. Transfer duck into a serving dish and decorate with pineapple rings on top.

(Above) A fruit stall in Campbell Street Market

(Above) A stall selling all types of Chinese food

DUCK IN PICKLED CABBAGE SOUP

1 whole duck (450 gm)
1/2 lb pickled cabbage (225 gm) cut into
  2 inches in lengths
4 tomatoes (cut into halves)

3 large onions(cut into halves)
A few whole peppers
2 slices sour fruit or use 2 slices of lemon
  for substitue

METHOD:

Wash duck and cut into joints, put whole peppers in a muslin bag and tie it into a knot. Boil 2 pints of water in a deep saucepan and add the duck.

After 10 minutes add the pickled cabbage, sour fruit or lemon slices, onions and whole peppers. Let muslin bag hang over the saucepan. Boil for a further 20 to 30 minutes and simmer for 10 minutes until duck is tender.

STEAMED DUCK WITH PINEAPPLE

Another popular dish is the Chinese people's favourite. Actually duck is only eaten on Chinese New Year's Day, because it is very expensive, so it is special. This is a delicious meal served with fried rice.

3 1b whole duck
1 small tin pineapple (already sliced)
A pinch of ground black pepper
A pinch of salt

1/2 teaspoon
  aji - no - moto (Gourmet Powder)
2 tablespoons vegetable oil
1 small cup of water

METHOD:

Chop duck into small portions, mix with pepper, salt and leave on one side for 5 minutes. Heat the oil in the wok until it is quite hot, over medium heat, add garlic and fry for about 2 minutes.

Add duck and stir fry for about 5 minutes, add water. Place duck on a large plate then onto a wire rack which will fit into the wok. Add enough water and cover wok with a lid and steam duck for about 20 minutes.
Heat half the oil in another pan and fry the pineapple, add aji - no - moto. Add steamed duck and simmer until tender.

HOW TO MAKE SAUCE:

2 teaspoons of cornflour
2 tablespoons of oyster sauce
2 tablespoons of water

Put oyster sauce in another small saucepan over low heat. Mix cornflour with a little water to a creamy texture and stir into the sauce. Add water and keep stirring until it bubbles, turn off heat.

Add this sauce to the duck and pineapple and stir well for a few minutes. Transfer duck into a serving dish and garnish with coriander.

EGG CURRY

5 eggs (medium size)
2 tablespoons vegetable oil
1 medium size onion (finely sliced)
1 teaspoon salt
1 dessertspoon cornflour
1/2 teaspoon cummin seeds
1/2 teaspoon turmeric powder
1/2 to 1 teaspoon red chilli powder
5 cloves garlic (finely sliced)

1 teaspoon coriander powder
1 large tin tomato
2 or 3 green chillies (finely sliced)
1/2 pint water
1 dessertspoon curry powder (optional)
1 dessertspoon sugar
A few sprigs of coriander leaves use for
  garnish (finely chopped)

METHOD:

Hard boil the eggs for about 5 to 6 minutes. Put eggs into cold water peel and put on one side.

Next peel and slice the onions and chillies. Wash coriander leaves and finely chop. Heat saucepan with the oil until quite hot, add the onions and stir for 1 to 2 minutes until light brown. Add all the spices and cornflour and stir well for a further 2 minutes to 3 minutes.

Then add the tomato and stir again for 2 minutes. Add water, salt then sugar and let it boil for about 8 to 10 minutes over medium heat. Finally add the eggs, coriander leaves, chillies and simmer for 5 minutes. Transfer onto a dish and serve. Add more salt if necessary. Served with boiled rice.

TIPS:

When using turmeric powder and red chilli powder, be careful with the stains, as it is hard to get stains off your clothes.

Egg Curry, Salad Dish and Yellow Rice

SIMPLE EGG OMELETTE

Makes 2 Servings

4 large eggs	2 tablespoons vegetable oil
1 red fresh chilli	A pinch of salt
1 medium onion (sliced)	A pinch of pepper
3 tablespoons milk	

METHOD:

Crack eggs into a large bowl and whisk it on speed 2 adding milk a little at a time. After that turn to speed 3 and whisk until fluffy. Put to one side.

Wash chilli and de-seed. Cut chilli into half legthways, then slice it finely. Peel onions and slice thin into rings. Add onions and chilli to the egg mixture and sprinkle salt and pepper. Mix it well with a fork.

Heat wok with oil until quite hot, over medium heat and pour egg into wok for 2 mins and then turn omelette over for 2 mins until light brown.

FRIED OYSTERS WITH EGG

This is another easy to make dish which can be used as a snack. In Malaya this snack is eaten in the evening of course you can eat it anytime you like.

For four persons:

2 lbs. Fresh Oysters (take meat out of shells)	4 tablespoons Oyster Sauce
6 medium size Eggs	1 tablespoon Dark Soya Sauce
5 cloves Garlic (chopped)	

Method:

Take Oysters out of shells wash and drain. Heat the grid with oil, add garlic while it is quite hot, throw in the oysters and stir well for 5 mins. Crack the eggs and stir in with the oysters. Start adding the oyster sauce and dark soya sauce and stir for another 10 mins. Add chilli sauce to oysters if preferred. Serve while it's still very hot.

It's a very mouthwatering dish.

STEAMED FISH IN OYSTER SAUCE

1 or 2 medium fish cod or trout
3 spring onions (diagonally sliced)
1 piece fresh ginger about 2 inch (finely sliced)

1 tablespoon oyster sauce
1 tablespoon vegetable oil
3 to 4 tablespoons water

METHOD:

Wash fish cut open and clean. Pat dry with kitchen paper. First put fish onto a plate and put a few slices of ginger inside the fish and on the top. Add 3 to 4 tablespoons of water to the fish.

Fill wok with two pints of water and then put a wire or wooden rack over it. Then place the plate onto the rack and cover the fish with lid. Steam for about 30 minutes until fish is tender.

When fish is cooked, it should look white in colour. Test it by pricking it with a fork. Transfer fish onto a dish.

Next heat a frying pan with 1 tablespoon of oil until hot, add the spring onions and oyster sauce and a tablespoon of water and stir fry for 1 minute. Turn off heat and pour sauce over the fish. Add more water if necessary so that it is not too dry.

TIPS:

Wire rack or cake tin stand can be used to stand the plate.

FISH WITH BROWN BEANCURD SAUCE (TOW CHEON SAUCE)

This is a sweet and sour dish, simple and quick to cook. Any fish can be used, eg trout, plaice or cod. Th fish may be cooked whole or cut into small pieces, and serve it with plain rice. This dish has a tangy flavour.

Ingredients:

1 lb fish 450 gm (trout, mackeral or plaice)
2 dessertspoons brown salted bean curd
 (tow cheon)
2 cloves of garlic (sliced)
1 shallot (sliced)
2 tablespoons vegetable oil
7 slices of ginger

1 piece of tamarind fruit (soaked in
 water for 5 mins and drained and
 reserve juice) discard the stones
1 fresh chilli (sliced)
1 dessertspoon of sugar
1 small bowl of water

METHOD:

Wash fish slit open gut and fillet. Heat wok with oil until hot, add ginger and fry for 1 min. Add garlic and shallot and stir well. After 2 or 3 mins. add 2 dessertspoons of bean curd (tow cheon) and stir for 1 min.

Next add 3 to 4 tablespoons of tamarind juice, then the sugar. After that add the fish. Stir fry for 3 mins and add slice chilli and a bowl of water and simmer for 5 mins. until fish is cooked.

TIPS:

Brown salted beans are sold in jars in Chinese supermarket also known as" Tow Cheon" in Chinese. Can be kept in fridge for up to 2 weeks.

SWEET AND SOUR FISH CURRY

This is a very special dish, because in Malaya it is eaten on a special occasion. Any fish but mackerel may be used, eg. trout is good and is normally steamed whole. Garnish with spring onions.

Ingredients:

2 to 3 tablespoons vegetable oil
10 shallots (peeled)
10 cloves of garlic (peeled)
2 or 3 stalks lemon grass (chopped)
1 lb 450 gm green ladies fingers (green
  vegetable shaped like fingers)
1 lb fish 450 gm (trout or mackeral)

Use 2 packet dry chilli powder or use
  fresh chilli paste
1 piece blachan about 2 inches (prawn paste)
1 pink curry flower (bunga kelantan) chopped
1 piece tamarind fruit (soaked in water for
  5 mins and drained, reserving the juice)

METHOD:

Wash fish and fillet. Wash ladies fingers and boil until soft and leave on one side. Heat oil in wok fry the chilli paste for about 5 mins then add chilli powder and stir for 2 mins. Add blachan (prawn paste) break into small pieces and stir. Add fish and keep stirring for a few mins then add tamarind juice and stir again.

Add more water if necessary. Boil for 5 to 8 mins and add pink chopped curry flower for the aroma. Finally add the whole ladies fingers and stir. Add sugar to taste. Simmer until fish is cooked.

TIPS:

Pink curry flower is known as "Bunga Kelantan" in Malayan language.
5 curry leaves could be used instead.

Stuffed Spicy Mackerels

STUFFED SPICY MACKERELS

Mackerels can be grilled or fried. The fish is used whole, but it needs gutting and the fins and head should be cut off. It is quite hot and spicy, it goes well with the rice and slices of cucumber. A cold drink may be needed as it quite hot!

2 medium size Mackerels
5 cloves garlic (chopped)
5 small shallots (peeled and sliced)
1 stalk lemon grass finely sliced or use
  1 tablespoon lime juice
1 inch (2.5 cm) yellow ginger (finely sliced)

6 dried chillies (soaked in water until
  soft then drained)
1 piece (1 inch/2.5 cm) Blachan (prawn
  paste) cut into small pieces
6 tablespoons of vegetable oil

METHOD:

First gut and fillet then slit both sides of the fish in the middle. Then blend all the ingredients together, garlic, lemon grass, shallots, chillies, yellow ginger and blachan (prawn paste) until the chilli paste is smooth. Add a little water if necessary.

Put 1 tablespoon of paste in the body and rub the remaining paste over the fish. Heat oil in wok until quite hot, add the fish and stir fry for 3 minutes each side until brown and cooked. Serve on a bed of rice.

SWEET AND SOUR FISH

2 large fish (450 gm)
1 egg
1 tablespoon cornflour
1/2 teaspoon salt
A pinch of pepper
1 teaspoon aji - no - moto
2 medium size onions (finely sliced)
2 tomatoes (sliced)

3 fresh red chillies (cut into 4 lengthways)
1 tea spoon chilli sauce
3 tablespoons tomato sauce
1 cup water
1 tablespoon vinegar
2 dessertspoons sugar
2 to 3 tablespoons vegetable oil
2 spring onions (chopped)

METHOD:

Wash, gut and cut fish into 2 inch pieces, season with cornflour salt and pepper. Mix 1 egg in a bowl with aji - no - moto with the fish and leave for about 20 minutes.

Heat the oil in the wok until quite hot on medium heat, add the fish and stir fry for about 4 minutes until light brown turning it over half way.

Then remove the fish from the wok and set aside. Stir fry the onions in the wok with tomatoes, chillies, tomato sauce for about 2 minutes. Add the vinegar, sugar, chilli sauce and water and boil for 5 minutes.

Mix cornflour with a little water to a creamy texture and add to the sauce. Continue stirring for 2 minutes, add salt and aji - no - moto to taste. Add fish and spring onions to the sauce and simmer for 3 minutes.

INDIAN FISH CURRY - LEMAK

This curry dish is cooked with a mixed curry powder. One tablespoon if you like it mild, two tablespoons if you like it hot. Madras curry powder can be used and served with plain rice.

5 cloves garlic (peeled and chopped)
1 lb fish 450 gm (mackerel or trout)
2 cups coconut milk
2 tablespoons tamarind juice (A 2 inch piece of tamarind soaked in water until dissolved, strained and reserve juice.)
2 tablespoons of curry powder or use half the amount if you prefer it mild
1 large onion (peeled and finely sliced)

4 tablespoons vegetable oil
A pinch of salt
1/2 lb (225 gm) ladies fingers (green vegetables shaped like fingers) finely sliced diagonally
3 spice powder (1/2 teaspoon of each cinnamon, star anise and cardamon)
2 tablespoons water

METHOD:

Soak tamarind in 1/2 a cup of water for 10 minutes, then drain and save the juice.
Wash fish, gut and fillet. Then cut fish into halves lengthways. Wash ladies fingers and cut diagonally.
Heat the oil in the wok until quite hot, add the onions and garlic and stir fry until light brown. Then add the curry powder and 2 tablespoons water and keep stirring for 5 minutes.

Add 3 spice powder that is cinnamon, star anise and cardamon. Stir again for 1 to 2 minutes. Boil for about 10 minutes over medium heat stirring constantly.

Add fish to the paste, stir for 1 minute, add tamarind juice and then turn down the heat a little before adding the coconut milk. Keep stirring, add ladies fingers to the curry. Let it simmer for about 10 minutes add salt to taste. Add more water if necessary.

TIPS:

Ladies finger is also known as "okra". It is available in any local supermarket. For coconut milk follow instructions at back of the packet.

STIR FRIED PORK WITH CAULIFLOWER AND CARROT

1/2 lb lean pork or prawns (frozen) or fresh

1 small cauliflower (cut into small pieces)

1 large carrot or 2 medium carrots (finely sliced diagonally)

3 to 4 cloves garlic (finely sliced)

1/2 teaspoon salt

1 tablespoon oyster sauce

2 to 3 tablespoons water

2 tablespoons vegetable oil

METHOD:

Wash carrots and cauliflower and cut into small pieces. Wash pork and pat dry and cut into thin strips.

Heat wok with oil until quite hot, add the garlic and stir fry until brown. Add the pork or prawns and stir fry for 5 to 6 minutes.

Next add the cauliflower and carrots and mix well, keep stirring vigorously for 6 to 8 minutes. Add oyster sauce and stir again then add water and let it simmer for 10 to 15 minutes until meat is tender. Add more water if necessary, finally add salt to taste.

STEAMED MINCED PORK

1/2 lb minced pork (225 gm)

1 large egg

1/2 teaspoon light soya sauce

1 teaspoon sugar

1/4 oz pickled brown beans (known as "Chye Poh" in Chinese) chopped

A pinch of pepper

A pinch of salt

METHOD:

Beat the egg in a bowl, then add the pork and stir well, add one teaspoon of water and mix. Put in the chopped pickled beans and soya sauce and stir with a fork, add salt and pepper to taste.

Next add sugar and then put meat mixture in a shallow dish and steam in a wok for about 15 to 20 minutes. It can be steamed after the rice is cooked and the heat is switched off. Place the dish on top of the rice and steam it that way. When it is steamed the meat should look white in colour instead of red.

Sweet and Sour Pork

STEAMED PORK WITH LADIES FINGERS

: lb ladies fingers or okras (450 gm)
·/2 lb minced pork (225 gm)
· large egg

2 desserspoons flour
1 teaspoon light soya sauce
1/2 teaspoon aji-no-mot

METHOD:

Wash ladies fingers and drain. Slit ladies fingers in the middle and set aside. Mix pork in a bowl with the egg, flour aji-nomoto and soya sauce together.

When it is well mixed put 2 teaspoons of the stuffing into the middle of the ladies fingers and steamed on a plate in the steamer for aout 15 minutes, making sure the water does not un dry.

SWEET AND SOUR PORK

· lb lean pork (450 gm)
· medium onion (cut into small squares)
1 green pepper (deseeded)
1 red pepper (deseeded)
1 small tin pineapple chunks
1/2 cucumber (finely sliced)

2 tablespoons tomato sauce
1 dessertspoon cornflour
1 tablespoon vinegar
2 tablespoons vegetable oil
1 dessertspoon sugar

METHOD:

Wash pork and cut into 1 inch cubes. Wash and deseed peppers and cut into small squares. Peel and cut onions into small squares. Mix cornflour with a little water to a creamy mixture.

Heat oil in wok until quite hot, add the onions and stir fry until light brown then add pork and stir fry for 5 to 6 minutes. Add pepper, cucumber, pineapple and juice.
Stir until well mixed for 5 minutes. Turn heat down a little and add the cornflour mixture and stir frequently. Next add tomato sauce and vinegar and stir again for 2 minutes.
Add sugar to taste and more water if necessary so that the sauce is not too thick. Serve with boiled rice.

PORK IN SOYA SAUCE

11b (450 gm) lean pork (cut into thin strips)
2 hard-boiled eggs (peeled and cut into quarters)
4 to 5 cloves garlic (peeled and finely sliced)
1 to 2 dessertspoons sugar
2 tablespoons vegetable oil
1/2 pint water

2 to 3 dessertspoons dark soya sauce
1/3 oz dried seaweed (soaked in water for 15
  minutes until soft and drained)
1/4 oz dried Chinese mushrooms (soaked in
  water for 25 minutes until soft and drained
  then sliced)

Pork in Soya Sauce with Chinese Mushrooms and egg

METHOD:

Hard boil the eggs for about 5 to 6 minutes. Put eggs in cold water to cool and then peel and cut into quarters. First heat the oil in a deep medium size saucepan until hot add garlic and stir fry for about 2 to 3 minutes until brown.

Next add the pork and stir for about 3 to 4 minutes, then add mushrooms and stir again for 1 minute. Add seaweed and dark soya sauce and stir frequently.

Add water and sugar to the meat and stir again for 1 minute. Add the eggs to the sauce and stir once more. Simmer for 5 minutes until meat is tender. Taste to see if more sugar or soya sauce is needed. Add more water if necessary.

TIPS:

Seaweed is black in colour, some are long and some are small flower shape.

SWEET AND SOUR RIBS

12 oz pork spare ribs (350 gm)	1 green pepper
1 cucumber	1/2 teaspoon garlic (chopped)
1 red pepper	1 small glass of wine (Red or White)
1 small onion (cut into squares)	1 tablespoon of vegetable oil

MARINADE FOR RIBS:

1 teaspoon soya sauce	A pinch of ground pepper
1/4 teaspoon salt	2 teaspoon cornflour
1/4 teaspoon sugar	

MARINADE FOR CUCUMBER:

1/2 teaspoon salt	1 tablespoon sugar
1/2 teaspoon rice vinegar	

SAUCE:

4 tablespoon vinegar	1/2 teaspoon soya sauce
1 tablespoon sugar	1/2 teaspoon cornflour (mix cornflour
1/2 teaspoon salt	with water to a creamy texture)
1/4 teaspoon of sesame oil	

METHOD:

Cut ribs into small pieces and marinade it for 30 mins. Heat the wok with oil until quite hot and deep fry the spare ribs over medium heat until meat is cooked. Drain off the oil. Cut red and green peppers into small pieces.

Wash cucumber and cut into half lenghtways and discard seeds. Cut into 5 cm. strips diagonally and marinade for 10 mins. Drain off and transfer onto a serving dish.

Heat 1 tablespoon oil in wok and saute garlic and onion on medium heat. Add wine and stir well. Then add the peppers and spare ribs and stir for about 10 mins. Mix sauce mixture and stir into the meat. Finally decorate spare ribs with cucumber and serve.

ROAST PORK

6 slices of lean pork
1 packet of red coloured powder
  (food colouring)

2 tablespoons light soya sauce
2 tablespoons sugar 3 to 4 cloves
  garlic (chopped)

METHOD:

Marinade pork in a casserole dish overnight. Rub meat with soya sauce and sprinkle with sugar. Add red powder over the pork and mix well. Add chopped garlic and stir. Cover it with a lid. Then refrigerate it overnight or you can marinate it 2 or 3 hours before grilling time.

Grill pork over charcoal fire on a skewer, keep turning every 5 minutes for at least 15 minutes. It can be done on a tray in the oven at gas mark 5, 315ºF, electric oven 190ºC for about 25 minutes. Test the meat to see if it is cooked by using a skewer to prick it. Basting is necessary during grilling time using the remaining marinade.

TIP:

Red powder, food colouring is sold in Chinese supermarkets and shops.

SPARE RIBS IN SOYA SAUCE

This popular dish is eaten by the Chinese people quite often. Chinese mushrooms can be added to give more flavour.

Serves 6 People

6 large spare ribs
2 tablespoon cornflour
6 cloves garlic (crushed)
1 inch piece ginger (2.5 cm) sliced

3 tablespoons dark soya sauce
2 glasses of sherry or white wine
2 dessertspoons sugar
1 small cup of water

Marinade

Method:

Rub meat all over with cornflour add garlic, ginger, dark soya sauce, wine and sugar and mix well in pyrex basin. Cover with a lid to marinate overnight in a fridge of for at least 3 hours before cooking.

Next day take the pyrex out of fridge and turn the meat over to the other side and then add 1 cup of water and cover with lid.

Place in slow oven for at least 3 hours at Gas Mark 3 (325ºF), (160ºC) until meat is tender.

TIPS:

If using more spare ribs, cook for an extra 30 minutes.

AUBERGINE WITH PRAWNS

1/2 lb prawns (225 gm)
2 medium size aubergines (finely sliced)
5 cloves garlic (chopped)
A pinch of salt

A pinch of pepper
1 fresh red chilli (finely sliced)
2 tablespoons vegetable oil
3 to 4 tablespoons water

METHOD:

Wash the aubergines and cut into half lengthways and finely slice. Wash the chillies, deseed and slice.

Heat the wok with oil until quite hot on medium heat, add the garlic and stir fry until light brown. Add the prawns and stir for 2 minutes, then add the aubergines and stir again for a further 3 to 4 minutes. Add salt and pepper and chillies to taste.

Add water to the aubergines and simmer for about 10 minutes until aubergines are soft.

STIR FRIED PRAWNS

Serves 4

8 oz prawns (225gm)
1 small brocolli (cut into small pieces)
4 oz beans (finely sliced) fresh or frozen
(optional) 100gm
1 dessertspoon cornflour (mix with a little
water into a creamy mixture)

1 tablespoon oyster sauce
2 tablespoons vegetable oil
3 to 5 cloves garlic (peeled and chopped)
or 1 medium onion (peeled and finely
sliced)

METHOD :

First mix the cornflour with 1 tablespoon water into a creamy mixture and set on one side. Wash brocolli and cut into small pieces. Heat the oil in a wok until quite hot on medium heat, add the garlic or onions and stir fry until light brown.

Reduce heat a little. Add the vegetables and stir fry for about 3 minutes and then add prawns, oyster sauce and stir again frequently for 10 minutes.

Sambal Udang (Prawns)
Stir fried mixed vegetable with rice

Add cornflour mixture to vegetables and keep stirring, add a little water if necessary so that sauce is not too thick. Simmer for about 5 minutes over low heat.

TIPS:

You may substitute dark soya sauce for oyster sauce.

SPICY PRAWNS WITH LONG GREEN BEANS

/2 lb long green beans cut into 2 inch pieces
/2 lb fresh peeled prawns
5 dried chillies, soaked in water until soft,
then drained

1 piece blachan (prawn paste)
6 small shallots or onions
2 stalks lemon grass (sliced fine)
2 inch piece yellow ginger (sliced) 5cm

METHOD:

Blend all the ingredients to a paste except prawns. Heat 2 tablespoons of oil in a wok until hot. Fry for 5 minutes until the paste is brown then add the green beans and stir for 6 minutes. Add the prawns and stir again for another 5 or 6 minutes. Add salt and 1 tablespoon of water and cook for a further 2 or 3 minutes. Taste to see it is not too dry, add more water if necessary. Serve on a bed of rice.

SPICY PRAWN WITH PINEAPPLE

1 lb (450 gm) king size prawns
1 large pineapple (peeled and sliced into
medium pieces)
6 shallots or small onions (sliced)
1 inch (2.5 cm) blachan (prawn paste) cut
into small pieces

1 stalk lemon grass (chopped) use 6 inches
from the bottom upward and discard the
rest of the stalks.
1 inch (2.5 cm) yellow ginger (sliced)
5 dried chillies or use fresh chillies (use
less if you prefer it mild)

METHOD:

Wash and peel prawns. Pound or blend all the ingredients except prawns into a smooth paste. Heat wok with oil until hot, add the chilli paste and fry for 2 to 3 mins. Turn heat down, and add the prawns and stir fry for 5 or 6 mins. Then add the pineapple pieces and continue stirring for 5 mins. Serve with boiled rice and cucumber salad.

This is a very hot and spicy dish. It is also mouth watering.

LADIES FINGERS WITH SPICY PRAWNS

1 lb (450 gm) ladies fingers (also known as okras) green vegetable shaped like ladies fingers.
1/2 lb (225 gm) fresh prawns
1 stalk fresh lemon grass (sliced) or use 2 tablespoon dried
1 inch piece blachan (prawn paste)

6 shallots or small onions (peeled and sliced)
1 inch piece yellow ginger (sliced)
6 dried chillies (soaked in water until soft, then drained)
5 cloves garlic (chopped)
2 tablespoons of water
2 tablespoons of vegetable oil

METHOD:

Wash and peel prawns. Wash ladies fingers and slice diagonally into 2 inch pieces. Using an electric blender on speed 2, to blend the ingredients, that is lemon grass, chillies, prawn paste, shallots, yellow ginger and garlic, except prawns and ladies' fingers. Blend it into a smooth paste. Switch off and stir with a spatula. Add a little water if necessary.

Heat oil in wok until hot, add the paste and stir until brown for about 5 minutes, then add ladies fingers , stirring frequently for about 8 minutes. Add water and mix well, add more water if necessary.

TIPS:

Lemon grass: Use 6 inches from the bottom and discard the rest. Or use 2 tablespoons dried lemon grass if fresh ones are not available.

PRAWN FRITTERS

4 oz of plain flour
1 large egg
A pinch of salt

A sprinkle of ground pepper
1 lb of fresh prawns or 1 tin (450 gms)

BATTER

To make the batter. Sift the flour twice into a bowl, crack an egg into the flour and use a mixer to beat it until it is creamy, add 3 tablespoons of milk and mix again for 2 mins. Add more milk (1 tablespoon) until you have a thick cream, add the salt and pepper, then the prawns and mix for about 1 minute.

Deep fry a spoonful of prawns in the fryer until brown and crispy, about 1/2 a minute each side and then lift out. Put it on a dish with napkin.

Makes about 12 - 14 fritters.

SAMBAL UDANG (SPICY PRAWNS)

used to watch my mother make this lovely spicy dish. Fresh unpeeled prawns are used for his dish. It is cooked with mixed curry pastes and sweet and sour tamarind juice. The prawn are added to the paste and tamarind juice gives a sweet and sour flavour.

lb Prawns (450 gm) unpeeled
peeled shallots (onions)
stalk finely sliced lemon grass
cloves of peeled garlic
inch finely sliced yellow ginger (2.5 cm)

1 inch blachan prawn paste (2.5 cm) cut
into small pieces
3 tablespoons tamarind juice
2 tablespoons vegetable oil

METHOD

Wash prawns and pat dry with kitchen paper. Blend shallots, lemon grass, garlic, yellow ginger and prawn paste into a smooth paste. Heat wok on medium heat until oil is hot. Add chilli paste and stir fry for 3 minutes until light brown, add prawns and stir fry for a further 5 minutes.

Soak tamarind fruit in a bowl for 10 minutes; after this squeeze fruit through a strainer and reserve the juice. Add 3 tablespoons of tamarind juice to the prawns and 1 tablespoon of sugar. Stir fry for 4 to 5 minutes until sauce gets quite thick. Serve with rice and cucumber.

TIPS

f fresh lemon grass is not available, you can substitute for 2 tablespoons of dried lemon grass or 1 tablespoon of grated lemon rind. Lemon grass is known as "serai" in Malaya.

LOH BAK SAUCE

1/2 bottle Buah Koh Cheung, black sweet sauce
1/2 bottle tomato sauce
2 tablespoon chilli sauce
4 pieces palm sugar known as "kong Tung",
special white rock sugar

1 tablespoon sesame seeds without
using oil fried until brown
A few drops of water
1 tablespoon granulated sugar

METHOD

Mix all the ingredients in a large deep bowl, add a few drops of water and sesame seeds and stir well. It is used specially for Loh Bak, pancake roll.

Hainanese Chicken Rice and Hainanese Chicken Soup

MARINADE SAUCE

2 teaspoons lemon juice
5 cloves garlic (finely sliced or chopped)
1 teaspoon soya sauce
1 teaspoon five-spice -powder

1/2 teaspoon turmeric powder
1/2 teaspoon sugar
1/2 teaspoon salt

METHOD:

Mix all ingredients in a bowl and stir well. Cut the meat into thin strips and mix the meat into the spice and cover with lid for at least two hours or overnight in refrigerator. Marinade sauce is use for soaking meat like chicken, beef, pork or lamb.

HAINANESE CHICKEN RICE

This popular dish, is different from the everyday plain rice which is cooked in the home. The Hainanese people like to cook their rice in chicken stock in order to improve the flavour. The rice is then served with the chicken slices and garnished with spring onions and as a side dish a small bowl of chicken soy and chilli sauce makes a wonderful meal.

There are many restaurants all over Malaya which sell Hainanese chicken rice. Perfect for complementing roast pork and roast duck.

4 cups of rice for 4 people
3 lb (1.5 kilo gm) chicken
1 pint chicken stock

METHOD:

Boil the rice in a deep saucepan with enough chicken stock to cover rice completely. Boil for 25 minutes, adding more stock if necessary. The rice will have a chicken flavour and should be soft and fluffy when cooked. It is served with a side dish of thick sliced cucumber and a plate of red chillies in soya sauce. It is also served with barbecued pork or roast chicken.

———— SOUPS ————

HAINANESE CHICKEN SOUP

8 tomatoes (sliced)
3 Ib (1.5 kg) whole chicken
2 spring onions - chopped

A pinch of salt
A pinch of pepper

Boil 2 pints (1.1 ltr) of water in a deep saucepan for 15 minutes. Whilst water is boiling, hold the chicken in the boiling water using two skewers for 25 to 30 mins, until the chicken is cooked. Remove the chicken from the water and place on one side to cool.

Switch off the heat from the saucepan and add salt and pepper to season the stock. When cool, cut the chicken into bite size pieces and arrange on a serving dish, sprinkle with chopped spring onions and decorate with tomato slices around the dish.

WANTAN MEE SOUP EGG NOODLE SOUP

Serves 4

1 lb (450 gm) fresh egg noodles or dried packets of noodles
1 to 2 lbs of pork ribs
1 lb lean pork (450 gm)
2 pints water
2 tablespoons red powder (food colouring for roast pork)
1 tablespoon sugar
1/2 teaspoon salt
1 tablespoon soya sauce

1/2 teaspoon aji-no-moto (gourmet powder)
12 wantan wrappers (3" x 3") square already made, available in Chinese Supermarket
1/2 lb minced pork, use for dumplings
3 to 4 green chillies (finely sliced and pickled with vinegar)
4 Chinese leaves, cut into 1 inch pieces
For garnish: use 1 to 2 chopped spring onions

METHOD:

Wash Chinese leaves and cut into 1 inch pieces and boil for 2 minutes and drain.

Rub lean pork with red food colouring all over both sides and add sugar, soya sauce and roast in oven for about 30 minutes until brown. When meat is cooked, cool and then slice it finely.

Place pork ribs into a deep saucepan with 2 pints of water and boil for about half an hour, adding salt and aji-no-moto to taste. Save the stock for later.

Boil noodles in another saucepan for about 2 minutes, drain and then rinse in cold water quickly and then back into boiling water, drain.

Divide noodles into 4 individual bowls. Serve with a few Chinese leaves, 3 dumplings and a few slices of roast pork. Add a few tablespoons of stock over the noodles and garnish with chop spring onions. Serve with pickled green chillies.

TIPS:

See recipe for Wantan Dumplings

Wantan Mee with roast pork and Chinese leaves

WANTAN MEE

SAUCE INGREDIENTS:

1 bottle light soya sauce to fill the pot
1 clay pot about 6 to 7 inches high
3 dessertspoon of aji - no - moto
3 dessertspoon of fish oil
Use another 6 to 7 inches pot

Fry pork oil first, then use oil to fill the
  second pot.
1 bunch Chinese leaves (wash and sliced
  into 2 inches)
1/2 lb of roast pork (finely sliced)

METHOD:

Boil egg noodles in hot boiling water for 2 mins, shake it, then dip into cold water and bring it straight out and dip back into hot water for 1 min. Drain the noodles.

Use one spoon of pork oil on the plate and one spoon of soya sauce which is already mixed in pot to put on plate. Then add the noodle and mix well with a pair of chop sticks. Serve with boiled Chinese leaves, wantan dumplings, roast pork slices.

WANTAN DUMPLINGS

1/2 lb minced pork
A pinch of aji - no - moto
1 small tin prawn 2 eggs
A pinch of salt

METHOD:

Use prawn and minced pork and mix in a large bowl. Add aji -no moto, salt to it and stir. Crack 2 eggs into the mixture and mix well. Use for fillings. Wantan skins can be bought in Chinese Supermarkets. Size 3 x 3 inch square.

PICKLED GREEN CHILLIES

2 lbs of green chillies (deseeded and sliced)
1 bottle of vinegar

1/2 dessertspoon of salt
1 dessertspoon of sugar

METHOD:

Wash chillies and take off the heads. Slice finely. Strain the chillies so that the seeds drop out. Put chillies in hot water for 2 mins. and then drain. Put chillies in a large jar and pour vinegar over it, add salt, and stir. It is ready in about 15 mins. for use.

HOW TO MAKE CHILLI PASTE

10 dried chillies (soaked in water until soft and drained) Remove the stalks from chillies
15 shallots (peeled)
1 inch piece (2.5 cm) yellow ginger (crushed and chopped finely)
6 cloves garlic (peeled)

2 stalks lemon grass (use 6 inches from the bottom upwards and finely chopped)
2 inch piece blachan (prawn paste cut into small pieces)
2 to 3 tablespoons vegetable oil

METHOD:

Blend all the ingredients except the oil in an electric blender into a smooth paste. Add a little water if necessary. Switch off and stir with a spatula.

Heat oil in wok until quite hot, stir fry the chilli paste until brown for about 5 to 6 minutes. Cool the paste and store in plastic container in refrigerator. Will keep for 2 to 4 weeks. Can also be kept in freezer.

HOW TO MAKE CHILLI SAUCE

1 lb (450 gm) fresh red chillies

METHOD:

Wash the chillies and remove the seeds and the green stalks before putting into the blender. Blend the chillies for 3 minutes until smooth. Put into plastic container and refrigerate. The sauce will keep for at least 2 weeks, can be frozen.

SWEET CORN AND CRAB SOUP

This is a starter soup dish which only takes 15 minutes to prepare. Only use a small bowl, as it can be quite filling. It takes delicious garnished with spring onions.

Serves 4
1 small tin sweet cream corn
1 to 2 tablespoons vegetable oil
2 to 3 spring onions (sliced diagonally)
2 egg whites (beat with a fork until frothy)
1 small tin crab

1 medium size onion (finely sliced)
1 dessertspoon cornflour (mix with a little water to a creamy mixture)
4 small cups of water
A pinch of salt
A pinch of ground pepper

METHOD:

Heat a deep saucepan with oil until quite hot, add the onions until brown for about 2 to 3 minutes over medium heat. Then add the crab and stir fry for 5 to 6 minutes.
Add enough water for 4 people and boil for 3 to 5 minutes. Turn heat down and slowly stir in the egg white.

(Above) A picture of two dragons at the Sleeping Buddha Temple in Penang

(Above) A father and son selling Durian fruits and Jack fruits

Keep stirring let it boil for about 3 minutes add sweet corn and then spring onions. Add salt and pepper to taste. Turn down the heat and finally add cornflour mixture to thicken the soup and simmer for about 5 minutes.

WANTAN SOUP

1/2 lb (225 gm) lean minced pork	1/2 teaspoon aji - no - moto
1 small tin crab meat	1/2 teaspoon light soya sauce
A pinch of salt	2 eggs

Put meat in a bowl and mix with crab meat, add aji - no - moto, salt, soya sauce and egg and mix well together. Use for wantan fillings.

PASTRY

1/2 lb wantan pastry (already made sold in packets in Chinese supermarket) 3" x 3" squares.
Or you can make it yourself 1/lb flour (sift twice)
1 or 2 egg
A pinch of salt

Mix flour in a bowl, crack eggs in the middle and whisk it until quite thick add the milk. Add salt and mix again for 1 min. and knead pastry on a floured board. Roll it fairly thin and cut into 3" x 3" squares. Makes about 16, use it for wrapping the meat.

Put one teaspoon of meat onto the centre of the pastry and gather it into the middle and seal with egg yoke or milk.

STOCK

1/2 lb spare ribs	A pinch of salt
A pinch of aji - no - moto	2 pints of water

Make stock by boiling spare ribs in a deep saucepan with water for about 30 mins. Add salt and aji - no - moto to stock. Drop wantan dumplings into the stock for 1 or 2 mins. and quickly bring it out of stock and drain. Put wantan dumplings into bowls and pour a small amount of stock over it, sprinkle with chopped spring onion.

OX-TAIL AND VEGETABLE SOUP

1 1/3 lb Frozen ox-tail (475gm)	2 Medium potatoes
2 oz Broad beans (5Ogm)	1 Medium onion
1 Carrot (sliced or grated)	2 Pints of water
3 Tomatoes	A pinch of salt

METHOD:

Thaw out the ox-tail and cut into small pieces. Boil it in a deep saucepan for about 30 minutes over medium heat. Wash the vegetables, peel carrots and slice, peel potatoes and cut into small pieces. Wash and peel broad beans. Wash tomatoes and cut into 4 quarters. Then peel onions and cut into 4. Boil all ingredients in a deep saucepan with water over medium heat. Add salt and taste then let it simmer for about 2 hours. Transfer soup into serving bowls. Garnish with corriander leaves.

MEAT AND VEGETABLE SOUP (CHAP CHYE TUNG)

1/2 lb of finely sliced liver (225 gm)
1/2 lb of finely sliced lean pork
1/2 lb cooked prawns (225 gm)
1/2 lb fish meat balls (225 gm)
1/2 Chinese white cabbage (225 gm)
1 medium onion finely sliced

1 teaspoon aji-no-moto
A pinch of salt
A pinch of ground pepper
2 pints of water (1.1 litre)
4 tablespoons vegetable oil

METHOD:

There is no need to wash fish balls.
Wash meat and finely slice. Wash Chinese cabbage cutting lengthways, into 2 inch strips. Peel and slice the onion.

Heat the wok until quite hot, add the onions, fry until light brown. Add liver stir for 2 minutes, add pork and stir 3 minutes. Add prawns and fish balls and stir again for 2 minutes, add Chinese cabbage.

Stir frequently add water and let it boil for 15 minutes. Sprinkle aji-no-moto, salt and pepper to taste. Simmer for a further 15 minutes.
Serve with boiled rice.
Chinese fish balls are sold in Chinese Supermarkets.

LENTIL SOUP

1 cup of lentils known as "dahl"
3 cups of water
1 teaspoon salt

1/4 teaspoon red chilli powder
2 tablespoons vegetable oil
1 or 2 cloves of garlic (finely sliced)

For garnish: use a few sprigs of fresh coriander leaves (chopped)

METHOD:

First rinse the lentils in cold water and then put through a strainer. Put all the ingredients with the water except the oil into a pressure cooker for about 7 to 10 minutes.

Switch off cooker. Heat another saucepan with oil until quite hot, add the garlic and stir fry until light brown.

Add the lentils and freshly chopped coriander to garnish. Simmer for about 10 to 15 minutes until soup is thick enough.

INDIAN CHICKEN SOUP

1 small chicken
3 cups water
1 large onion, cut into halves (peeled and finely sliced)

1 clove garlic (peeled and finely sliced)
2 tablespoons vegetable oil
1 teaspoon salt

METHOD:

Wash the chicken and cut into joints. Put chicken in a saucepan with 3 cups of water, and half the onion and garlic. Add 1 teaspoon salt and boil over low heat for about 1 hour.

When the meat is very soft, remove the chicken and reserve the stock. Remove meat from bone and mash the chicken.

Use another saucepan to heat the oil, when oil is hot, add half the finely chopped onion and stir fry until light brown. Add stock to the onion mixture.

After boiling for about 10 minutes, strain the soup and then add the chicken meat and simmer on low heat for 5 minutes.

BEAN CURD SOUP

2 square white bean curds or use 1 carton of beancurd
2 to 3 cloves garlic (peeled and chopped)
1/3 oz dried seaweeds (soaked in water until soft, then drained)
1/2 lb (225 gm) prawns or use lean pork (finely sliced)
1/4 lb fresh white fish balls (sold in packets in Chinese supermarkets)
4 oz Chinese mushrooms (soaked in water until soft then drained and sliced)
1 dessertspoon brown pickled beans (already chopped) also known as "Tung-Chye"
2 tablespoons vegetable oil
1/2 teaspoon aji - no - moto (Gourmet Powder)
1/2 teaspoon salt
3/4 pints of water

Sweet corn and Crab soup with spring onions and
Mee Goreng Stir fried Noodles (above)

Bean-curd soup with sea-weed (bottom)
Stir Fried Green Beans with prawns (top)

METHOD:

Cut bean curds into 2 inch pieces. Heat oil in a deep saucepan until quite hot, add the garlic and stir fry until brown for about 2 to 3 minutes.

Add pork or prawns and stir for 3 to 6 minutes then add seaweed and pickled beans to the meat.

Add Chinese mushrooms, fish ball, salt and stir for 1 to 2 minutes then add 3/4 pints of water and let it boil over medium heat for about 15 to 20 minutes. Add aji - no - moto to taste.

VEGETABLE SOUP

1 pint of vegetable stock (600 ml)
1 small cauliflower (cut into small pieces)
1 medium carrot (finely sliced)
A pinch of salt

2 tablespoons vegetable oil
1/2 teaspoon Aji - no - moto
3 cloves garlic (chopped)
1/2 lb Chinese cabbage

METHOD:

Wash cabbage and cut into 2 inch lengths.

Heat a deep saucean with the oil and stir fry the garlic until light brown. Add stock and boil for about 30 minutes. During boiling add salt and aji - no - moto to taste.

Add carrots, cauliflower and Chinese cabbage to the stock and simmer for 5 to 6 minutes.

ABALONE FISH SOUP

1 tin Abalone fish sliced
1 small tin peas or a few lettuce leaves
  cut into 2 inch lengths
A pinch of salt

1 pint of water
1/2 teasoon Aji-no-moto, gourmet powder
2 cloves chopped garlic
1 - 2 tablespoons vegetable oil

METHOD:

Heat oil in the wok until quite hot and then stir fry garlic until light brown.

Add the water and boil for 10 minutes, then add salt, aji-no-moto to taste, then add Abalone fish and stir for 3 minutes.

Add the peas or lettuce and simmer for 5 minutes.

PORK IN MUSHROOM SOUP

1 lb pork ribs finely sliced (450 gm)
8 oz mushrooms finely sliced (Chinese
   mushrooms soaked in water until soft
   and drained
4 medium potatoes

2 tablesoons vegetable oil
A pinch of salt and peer
1/2 teaspoon aji-no-moto
1 clove chopped garlic
3/4 pint of water

METHOD:

Heat saucepan with oil and stir fry garlic until golden brown.
Add pork and stir fry for 3 minutes.
Add the mushrooms and stir again, then add water and boil for about 10 minutes.
Peel and cut potatoes into 4 and add to the stock.
Add salt, pepper and aji-no-moto to taste.
Boil meat for a further 15 minutes.

TIPS:

If you can not get fresh mushrooms use a tin of mushrooms

FISH BALL SOUP

1 tablespoon vegetable oil
1 medium sliced onion
1/2 clove chopped garlic
1/2 teaspoon aji-no-moto
1 packet fish balls
2 or 3 leaves of spinach or Chinese
   cabbage or lettuce

1 carrot finely grated
1 tablespoon light soya sauce
A pinch of salt
2 chopped springs onions
1 pint of water

OPTIONAL

1/4 oz sea-weed, soaked in water until soft and drained

METHOD:

Cut vegetables into 1 inch pieces.
Heat oil in saucean until hot, stir fry onions until golden brown.

Add water and boil for 8 minutes then add vegetables.
After that add fish balls, soya sauce, salt and spring onions.
Add aji-no-moto and boil for about 10 minutes.

TIPS:

Fish balls can only be found in Chinese shops.

LOH BAK (MINCE MEAT IN PANCAKE ROLL)

Makes 12 pancake rolls

3 large bean curd wrappers
1 lb bang kuang (A round vegetable like
  swede, has a sweet taste)
1 large onion (finely sliced)
5 cloves garlic (chopped)
1/2 teaspoon aji - no - moto (Gourmet
  Powder)
A pinch of salt

1 spring onion (chopped)
1/2 lb mince pork (225 gm)
4 oz mushrooms (peeled and finely sliced)
1/2 lb beansprouts (wash and drained)
1/2 tablespoon red coloured spice powder
1/2 tablespoon sugar
1 dessertspoon cornflour
4 medium size egg yolks
1 pint vegetable oil for deep frying

METHOD:

Mix all ingredients in a large bowl that is all the vegetables with the spice. Add 1/2 tablespoon sugar, egg yolks and cornflour together. Add a pinch of salt, aji - no - moto and red powder to the mixture and stir well.
Heat the oil in the wok until hot add the onion and stir fry for 1 to 2 minutes add the garlic and stir until light brown.

Add the mincemeat and stir fry for 2 to 3 minutes then add spring onions, mushrooms and beansprouts. Continue stirring for 8 to 10 minutes. Simmer until vegetables are very soft and meat is cooked. Turn off heat and put vegetables to one side.

Bean curd wrappers can be bought already made in Chinese Supermarket. It has to be cut into 5" x 5 square. Put one dessertspoon of vegetable mixture onto the middle of the square and roll forward once. Fold in left side, then fold in right side and roll forward once and seal with cornflour. Mix cornflour with a little water for sealing.

DEEP FRYING

Heat oil in wok until very hot before deep frying. Drop the pancake in for 1 to 2 minute each side until brown.

TIPS:
If fresh bean curd is not available, use dried ones. Need to soak in water until soft before using.

Man making rice papers for spring rolls

SPRING ROLLS - PENANG STYLE (POH PEAH)

Makes 10

1/2 lb fresh prawns or use cooked prawns
3 or 4 crabs (or use 1 tin of crab)
1/2 lb beansprouts
1 Bang Kuang (it is a round vegetable
and tastes like swede) peeled and finely
sliced

2 yellow bean curds (squares, cut into
small pieces) Optional 1 large onion
finely sliced
10 rice papers for wrapping (available in
Chinese Supermarket)
2 pints of water
3 to 4 tablespoons vegetable oil

METHOD:

Wash beansprouts and drain.

Boil prawns in water for 10 minutes and save the stock for later use. Drain and peel prawns. If using fresh crab, boil crabs for 15 or 20 minutes until the shell turns pink, then it is cooked. Drain crabs and leave to cool.

Mash crab meat in a bowl and set on one side with the prawns.

Wash and slice the vegetables finely. Heat the wok with 3 or 4 tablespoons of oil. When hot add onions and stir fry until light brown (medium heat).
Then add Bang - Kuang, beansprouts and stir for 5 minutes. Then adding prawns, crabs, beancurds and stir for another 8 minutes.

Add salt, pepper and half a pint of stock and simmer for about 20 minutes until vegetables are soft.

RICE WRAPPERS

Put 1 dessertspoon of vegetables onto the rice wrapper roll forward once. Then fold in left and right sides and roll forward to the end and seal with cornflour.
Brush springrolls with chilli or tomato sauce.

VEGETARIAN SPRINGROLLS

Makes 12

2 medium onions, peeled and
finely sliced
3 carrots, finely grated
8 oz Chinese mushrooms, soaked
in water until soft and finely slice

1 whole bangkuang which looks
like a turnip, white round vegetable
or 1/4 lb green beans, finely sliced
2 tablespoons vegetable oil

METHOD:

Wash all vegetables and finely slice, onions, bangkuang and mushrooms. Wash beansprouts and drain, grate the carrots.

If green beans are used finely slice.

Heat wok on moderate heat until oil is quite hot, add onions, stir fry for a few minutes until light brown. Add bangkuang, mushroom and beansprouts, stirring for about 10 minutes until well mixed, add salt to taste.

Put one dessertspoonful of vegetables onto the middle of the wrapper. Roll forward once, then fold left and right sides in and roll forward to the end. Seal with cornstarch before deepfrying.

MAKING THE SAUCE

Ingredients:

1 tablespoon tomato sauce	1 tablespoon lime juice
1 tablespoon chilli sauce	1 tablespoon granulated sugar
1 tablespoon oyster sauce	

METHOD

Mix tomato, chilli, oyster sauces, lime juice and sugar into a saucepan. Cook over medium heat for 5 minutes until bubbling, keep on stirring and then pour sauce into a bowl. Can be used as a dip or can be poured over the top of pancake rolls.

ROTI - CHENAN - INDIAN PANCAKE

1/2 tablespoon sugar	6 oz self-raising flour
A pinch of salt	1/4 pint milk
2 large eggs	1 tablespoon vegetable oil

METHOD:

Sift flour into a bowl three times. Put flour into a mixing bowl add salt and crack an egg one at a time in the bowl and mix on speed 2.

Add milk a little at a time and mix again for 2 minutes. Add more milk if necessary so that it is not too thick.
Sprinkle flour on board and knead the dough several times. Put on one side for about half an hour to rise.

Samosas and Vegetarian Spring Rolls

After that knead once or twice and then take about 2 inches of dough and roll it flat. Use a grid or a frying pan and add 1 tablespoon oil until hot, add the pancake mixture and fry until brown 2 to 3 minutes on each side.

Roti-chenan is a pancake normally eaten with any curry dish or dahl served with a side dish of slice onions rings soak in one tablespoon of white vinegar.

SAMOSAS (INDIAN STYLE)

Fillings:

1/2 lb mince meat	2 or 3 green chillies (finely sliced)
1/2 teaspoon red chilli powder	1 dessertspoon cummin seeds
1 teaspoon salt	1 medium size onion (finely sliced)
1/4 teaspoon turmeric powder	2 to 3 tablespoons vegetable oil
1 inch fresh yellow ginger (finely sliced)	

METHOD:

Heat the frying pan with oil until quite hot. Add the meat and salt and stir well. Add all the dried spices and stir fry for about 15 to 20 minutes until meat is cooked on medium heat.

PASTRY:

1 cup of self-raising flour	1 teaspoon baking powder
1 teaspoon oil	2 to 3 tablespoons of milk
1/4 teaspoon salt	

METHOD:

Mix all the ingredients in a mixing bowl on speed 2 to make into quite a thick dough. Add a little bit of milk at a time.

Sprinkle flour on the board and knead the dough a few times. Cut into small balls and roll it flat and not too thin. Then cut the round shape into half the size.

Use one half only, fill with 1 dessertpoon of meat onto the pastry and fold into a triangle sealed pastry with milk. Repeat with all the pastry and deep fry in hot oil until brown. Drained onto the greaseproof paper to dissolve the oil. Only deep fry for about 2 minutes each side.

CHAPATTIS (INDIAN PANCAKE)

8 oz brown flour	1/4 oz cold water

METHOD:

Sift flour into a bowl. Mix with small amounts of water at a time and knead like a dough. Roll into a small ball and roll into a flat, round shape. Using a grid on the stove, wait until hot, then add some oil to the grid pan. Put the dough onto the grid and flatten for a few minutes on each side until brown.

These Chapattis are eaten with mixed vegetable and curry dishes.

TIPS:

When chapattis are cold, sprinkle with some cold water and put under the grill for 1/2 a minute each side.

INDIAN SALAD DISH

METHOD:

Make a plate of mixed vegetable salad to go with the dish. Use one small carton of natural yoghurt, whisking before serving with the curry dish. This salad is eaten with curry, chicken or lamb, together with cucumber, sliced tomatoes, sliced onions, pineapples etc. Sprinkle with 1 tablespoon vinegar.

——— DESSERTS ———

PANDAN CAKE

Pandan comes from the name of the leaf. These leaves grow on a small bush. They are 2 feet long and it is green in colour. The leaves are used for their aroma and the juice of the leaf is used for cooking and especially for making cakes. The leaves are tied in knots and dropped in the saucepan for steaming. The taste is very appetizing. This gives a light green colouring.

8 oz plain flour (225 gm)
1 teaspoon baking powder
1/2 teaspoon bicarbonate soda
A pinch of salt
5 egg yolks
3 fluid oz corn oil (85 ml) or use
   3 oz margarine

5 egg whites
1/4 teaspoon of cream of tartar
8 oz caster sugar (225 gm)
Green food colouring
8 Pandan leaves or use any essence
   if preferred
2 fluid oz water (50 ml)

METHOD:

First wash Pandan leaves and add 2 oz of water, squeeze out the juice from leaves and strain discarding the leaves. Cream egg yolks and half the sugar until thick, stir in the corn oil and pandan juice. Fold and sift flour (three times) into egg mixture. Then add green colouring to desired colour.

Stir well to mix evenly. Whisk egg whites until fluffy, add the remaining sugar in small amounts and beat until stiff. Fold into the egg yolk mixture quickly. Bake in preheated oven 325°F or Gas Mark 3, 160°C for about 50 minutes until firm to touch. Use a skewer to test it by pricking in the centre of the cake.

If Pandan leaves are not available you can use green food colouring. You can also use any flavouring to suit yourself.

COCONUT SPONGE CAKE

5 oz self-raising flour	1 packet dessicated coconut (sweet)
5 oz margarine	1 jar glace cherries (100gm)
5 oz granulated sugar	A pinch of salt
3 large eggs	1 or 2 tablespoons milk

METHOD:

Warm mixing bowl in oven on low heat for 10 mins. Sift flour three times in a bowl. Put margarine in warm mixing bowl and whisk until soft. Add sugar and whisk for 3 mins. Crack one egg at a time and whisk until fluffy. Then add flour and whisk until quite fluffy. Add milk 1 tablespoon at a time to mix well.

Add dessicated coconut and whisk again for 2 mins add salt. Transfer mixture into a round lined 8 inch cake tin and put in the oven on Gas Mark 3, 325° F, 160° C for 60 mins. Cool it on rack and decorate cake with cherries.

TIPS:

Test it by using a pallette knife to touch the top of the cake to see if it is firm or when cake leaves the side of the tin.

BANANA CAKE

6 oz self-raising flour (175 gm)	2 medium bananas
6 oz granulated sugar (175 gm)	A pinch of salt
6 oz margarine (175 gm)	1 to 2 tablespoons milk
3 large eggs	

METHOD:

Sift flour in bowl three times. Peel bananas and discard the skins. Cut bananas into 4 or 6 pieces. Warm the bowl in the oven. Add the margarine and whisk for about 2 minutes until margarine is soft.

Add eggs one at a time, whisk until fluffy on speed 2. Add sugar and whisk again for 1 minute then add flour and whisk again for 2 minutes. Add a little milk and salt and keep whisking for a further 2 minutes add banana until it is creamy.

Glutinous Rice Cake

Line an 8 inch cake tin with greaseproof paper and pour the cake mixture into the tin and bake in the middle of the oven for about 50 minutes on Gas Mark 3, 325°F, 160 C.

TIPS:

To find out if cake is cooked, test it by using a pallette knife to touch the top of the cake to see if it is firm. It can be also cook in a microwave oven for about 8 minutes. Cake does not get brown in microwave oven.

GLUTINOUS RICE CAKE

4 cups of glutinous rice
2 cups of coconut milk

1/2 lb (225 gm) sugar
Food colouring use blue or leave it white

METHOD:

Wash the rice and drain. If using dried coconut milk mix with two cups of water. Boil the rice in a deep saucepan for 30 to 40 minutes until double in size.

The rice can be steamed in a steamer on a low heat for 1 and a half hour. Make sure that water does not run dry. Always add more water.

Next add sugar and colouring and stir well until colour is mixed properly.

Test to see if rice is cooked. Taste it to see if it is soft. Then switch off cooker. Empty rice into a big plate and let it cool. Put in the fridge for 1 hour and cut into diamond shapes.

BO BO CHA CHA PUDDING

1 large yam
1 medium sweet potatoes (cut into bite
  size pieces)
1/4 lb black eyed beans (soaked overnight)
  discard the skins

3 bananas (sliced)
4 tablespoons granulated sugar
2 pints coconut milk
1/4 oz sago

METHOD:

Peel yam and cut into bite size pieces. Peel sweet potatoes and cut into small pieces and steam with the yam for about 3 minutes.
Put sago into a bowl and pour boiling water over it, stir it first with a fork . Then add some flour to knead the sago into long strips, and cut into small pieces.
Put sago in a small saucepan to boil for 1 or 2 minutes and then strain. Put sago in a bowl of cold water and then drain. Boil 2 - 3 pints of coconut milk in another large saucepan with 2 pandan leaves (tied in knots).

Finally drop yam, sweet potatoes, blacked eyed beans, bananas, sago and sugar into the saucepan of coconut milk and boil for about 10 minutes. Add sugar to taste.

SEMOLINA OR SAGO PUDDING

Serves 4

4 oz semolina (100 gm)
4 oz granulated sugar (100 gm)
1 thick cup of coconut milk

1 and 1/2 pints of water (900 ml)
2 bananas (sliced diagonally)
1 medium sweet potatoe (peeled)

METHOD:

Peel potatoes and cut into small pieces. Boil the semolina with the water in a deep medium saucepan for 25 to 30 minutes on medium heat. After 15 minutes, reduce the heat.

Boil the semolina until it swells double in size and that the potatoes are soft. During cooking, add the sugar and keep stirring so that it is not lumpy. In the last 5 minutes add the bananas. Served with one tablespoon of thick coconut milk on the top of the semolina. It has a creamy sweet taste.

BLACK RICE PUDDING

Serves 4

8 oz black rice (225 gm)
4 oz sugar (100 gm)

1 and 1/2 pint water (900 ml)
1 cup thick coconut milk

METHODS:

Wash the rice and put into a deep saucepan with cold water. Cover with a lid and boil for about 30 to 40 minutes until the rice has doubled in size.
When the rice starts boiling, open the lid half-way to let steam out. After 15 minutes turn heat down a little to simmer. Add sugar and stir for a few minutes. When rice is cooked, put into individual bowls and sprinkle 1 to 2 tablespoons of thick coconut milk on top of it.

TIPS:

Black rice is available in any Chinese supermarket.

PANCAKE (PENANG STYLE) (BANG CHANG KOAY)

6 oz self-raising flour
1 dessertspoon sugar

3 to 6 tablespoons water
4 oz margarine 1 or 2 eggs (optional)

METHOD:

Sift flour three times in a mixing bowl. Mix flour with sugar, then add water and mix well. Make sure it is not too thick and sticky. Add more water if necessary.

Chinese Man selling Penang Pancake

Heat the omelette pan and then brush with a bit of oil. Pour a small amount of batter into pan and shake it round so that it spread out and cover the pan. Leave for 2 to 3 mins. to cook until it rises and look fluffy.

Then brush the pancakes with margarine and sprinkle lots of peanuts all over the pancakes. Leave it for a further 1 or 2 min. and then use a palette knife to go round the sides and lift it up and fold the pancakes into half by pressing it.

HOW TO MAKE PEANUT MIXTURE:

8 oz of chopped peanuts   4 oz of granulated sugar

Mix peanuts and sugar in a bowl. Use for filling the pancake. If using whole peanuts, put into blender and blend with the sugar until it is all chopped up.

BANANA FRITTERS

Serves 4

4 bananas   A pinch of salt
4 oz plain flour   1 small tin golden syrup
1 egg large   1 litre vegetable oil
2 to 3 tablespoons milk

METHOD:

Peel the bananas and then cut into half lengthways.

TO MAKE A BATTER:

Sift flour into a bowl three times. Put flour in a mixing bowl and crack an egg into the centre of the bowl. Mix on speed 2 for 2 minutes then add milk a little at a time. Add more milk if necessary, to that it is not too thick.

Put bananas into the bowl and turn the bananas over until well coated. Heat the deep-fryer until quite hot, before putting in the bananas two or three at a time until golden brown. Turn bananas over once and drain the bananas onto the paper towel on plate to absorb the oil.

Heat the golden syrup in a small saucepan until runny and pour over the bananas.

PINEAPPLE VOLCANO

Makes 4

4 medium pineapples
Ice-cream (any flavour)
1 large tin mixed fruit cocktail or use fresh fruits
1 packet mixed chopped nuts

4 small candles
1 bar dark chocolate (grated)
1 carton double whipped cream

METHOD:

Cut the top of pineapple, scoop out all the pineapple. Place pineapple onto a plate. Put one scoop of ice-cream into the pineapple then add fruits, nuts, cream and repeat twice.

On the top sprinkle nuts, chocolate syrup and place a small flat candle for decoration on top and light the candle.

ICE - KACHANG (CRUSHED ICE WITH JELLY & ICE-CREAM)

Makes 4

1 tin sweet cream corn
1/2 lb (225 gm) sweet red beans
  (boiled until soft)
1/4 lb (114 gm) small jar of (Atap-chi)
  small minature fruit like coconuts.

1 small tin of carnation milk
3 different coloured syrup
1 packet of jelly (put in individual moulds)
Ice-cream (1 scoop for each dish)
Crushed ice (1 large bowl)

METHOD:

Crush the ice into a large bowl. Divide into 4 individual bowls. Then fill the bowls with red beans, sweet corn, atap-chi and cover with crushed ice.

Sprinkle ice with 3 different coloured syrups and add jelly and 1 scoop of ice-cream on the side.

ROJAK SPICY MIXED FRUIT SALAD

2 or 3 small red Jambus (small sweet
  fruit taste like strawberries)
1/2 sliced cucumber
1 teaspoon red chilli sauce

1 small fresh pineapple cut into small pieces
1 tablespoon black/brown prawn paste
2 small green mangoes
1 large star fruit (sliced)

METHOD:

Wash all the fruit, cutting the jambus into 4 pieces, slice the mangoes, taking out the stones. Put the fruits into a bowl, adding the black prawn paste and chilli sauce. Stir well.

To make the sauce

1 tablespoon crushed peanuts
2 tablespoons soya sauce
1 tablespoon boiling water
2 fresh chillies sliced very finely

1/2 cup boiling water
tablespoon sugar
1/2 teaspoon dried shrimp paste (blachan)

METHOD:

Mix ingredients together and pour over the fruit salad (optional).

RAMBUTAN JAM

Makes 1 jar
1 lb rambutans (450 gm) peeled
1 lb granulated sugar (450 gm)

1 packet arrow root gelatine
1 tablespoon water

METHOD:

Peel rambutans and discard skins. Cut rambutans into 4 quarters and take out the stones. Cut rambutans into half again, so that they are smaller pieces.

Rinse rambutans using a strainer, the white fruit inside looks like coconuts. Heat a deep saucepan with a tablespoon of water over low heat, add the rambutans and stir for 5 minutes. Then add the sugar and stir again.

Stirring frequently, and when rambutans start to get soft, boil it for about 20 minutes. Then turn heat down and add gelatine. Continue stirring all the time until jam gets quite thick.

Test it by putting a bit of jam on a saucer to see how thick it is. Then switch off and pour jam into a warm jar and seal with lid.

(Above) Trishaws in busy Penang Road

(Right) A Burmese Temple at The Sleeping Buddha in Penang

TIPS:

Wash jar and lid and warm on a tray in oven on low heat for 5 to 10 minutes. Gas Mark 1, 275°F, 140°C.

Rambutan is a small hairy fruit and the skin is green and turn into red when it is ripe. The fruit is white and looks like little coconuts. It is quite easy to peel and it taste very sweet. There is a big stone in the middle, do not eat stone.

STAR FRUIT JAM

Makes one jar
1 or 2 tablespoons water
1 lb/450 gm star fruits

1 lb/450 gm granulated sugar
1 packet arrowroot gelatine

Wash star fruits and slice thinly into star shapes. Alternatively slice into long strips and cut into smaller pieces. Remove small stones with a fork and discard. First heat in a deep saucepan with a tablespoon of water over a low heat. Add star fruits and stir for 5 minutes, then add all the sugar, keep stirring for a further 5 minutes. When fruits start to soften, boil for 20 minutes over a medium heat. Turn the heat down low, add the gelatine and continue stirring until the jam thickens. Test by putting a sample of the jam onto a saucer and judge how sticky it is. Switch off the heat and pour the jam into warmed jar, sealing the lid.

TIPS:

Wash jar and lid and warm on a tray in the oven on a low heat (Gas Mark 1/275 deg F/140 deg.cent.)

PINEAPPLE JAM

Makes one jar
large pineapple
1 lb granulated sugar

1 packet arrow root (gelatine)
1 tablespoon water

METHOD:

Cut off the top and bottom of the pineapple. Peel pineapple and core it. Slice pineapple very finely.

Heat a deep saucepan with a tablespoon of water over low heat. Add the pineapple slices and sugar and stir for 5 minutes.

When pineapple start to get soft, boil it over medium heat for about 20 minutes. Then turn down the heat and add gelatine and continue stirring all the time until jam gets quite thick.

Test it by putting a bit of jam on a saucer to see how thick it is. Switch off cooker and pour am into warm jar and and sealed with lid.

TIPS:

Wash jar and lid and warm jar on a tray over low heat in over Gas Mark 1, 275°F, 140°C.

KAYA (COCONUT JAM)

10 large eggs	2 and 1/2 whole coconut milk (do not mix with water)
1 lb sugar (450 gm)	4 or 5 pandan leaves

METHOD:

Whisk eggs with sugar on speed 2 until fluffy and that sugar is dissolved. Add coconut milk and continue whisking for 3 to 5 minutes until creamy.
Wash pandan leaves and tie into knots, put egg mixture and leaves into the steamer and steam for about 15 minutes on medium heat. Cover with brown paper and then with lid before steaming.

After 15 minutes remove steamer from heat and whisk jam for about 3 minutes, return back to cooker. Repeat again every 25 minutes again .

After whisking 5 times, take pandan leaves out and discard. This time steam for about 5 hours in total. Switch off cooker, pot the jam and sealed with lids. Can keep in refrigerator for up to 2 weeks.

TIPS:

For steaming use a steamer, or a wok.

COCONUT DRINK

Young coconuts are picked for its milk. To test if the coconuts are young or old, young coconuts are green and when shaken the liquid can be heard. If the coconut is old it means there is not much milk.

Chop the top of the coconut off. Make a big hole so that you can use a straw to suck the juice. After that you can use the spoon to scoop out the white flesh.
Scoop out all the white flesh, put into tall glasses, add 1 tablespoon of sugar syrup (optional). Add all the coconut juice and a few ice-cubes in glasses. Wet the edge of the glass with water, then sprinkle with sugar. Now it's ready to serve.

STAR FRUIT DRINK

Star fruit are oval shape fruits, yellow in colour, very juicy and crispy. It can be obtained from local supermarket.

Wash 1 or 2 star fruits. Slice them about 1/2 inch thick. Put 1 tablespoon of syrup in each glass top with star fruit juice. To make the juice, put star fruit in blender and blend for 1 or 2 mins. discard the fruits. Put through a strainer. Pour juice into glasses.
Wet the edge of the glass with water, and sprinkle some sugar. Put a few ice-cubes into glasses and serve.

FRESH ORANGE DRINK

4 large oranges for 4 persons
4 tablespoon sugar syrup
Ice-cubes

Cut oranges into halves. Squeeze juice of each orange into tall glasses. Add 1 tablespoon sugar syrup in each glass and stir well. Fill up with ice-cubes and serve with straw.

HOW TO MAKE SUGAR SYRUP

1 lb. sugar (450 gm.)
1 - 1/2 pint of cold water

Boil water in a deep saucepan with the sugar for about 20 mins. until sugar has dissolved and quite thick and syrupy. Switch off. Cool the syrup and store in a glass jar or container. It is used especially for making drinks only.

SUGAR CANES

Sugar canes are grown throughout the whole of Malaya. Sugar is made from sugar cane. There are 3 types: the first one is the yellow coloured skin, the second is the purple colour and the last one is a mixed colour which is used for making tea. It is about 6 feet tall and slim. When it is ripe, the branch is quite thick. The original colour of sugar is light brown and when it is refined it turns into white. Refined sugar is much sweeter than the brown one. When the sugar cane is ripe, chop it from the bottom, then chop the top leaves off. The whole sugar cane can be cut down to 6 sections and it is then put through a machine known as the "Mangle" to squeeze out all the juice. It is then put through a muslin or a strainer. It tastes refreshing when it's cold.

Sugar cane is then delivered to the factory to be made into sugar and packed for export.

A sugar cane drinks stall

HOT SUGAR CANE TEA

This tea taste refreshing.

2 stalks sugar canes
  6 to 8 oz granulated sugar or use less if preferred
2 pints water

METHOD:

Chop off both ends of the sugar canes. Then peel off the skins and cut into small pieces. Put sugar cane into a large deep saucepan with the water and boil for about 30 minutes with the sugar. Turn off heat.

After boiling. drain the sugar canes and discard, saving just the tea. Pour hot tea into a muslin bag and filter through before drinking.

PINEAPPLE DRINKS

Makes 4

1 medium size pineapple
1/4 pint water
1/2 pint pineapple juice

4 tablespoons sugar syrup
Ice cubes

METHOD:

Cut off the top and bottom of the pineapple. Peel and cut into pieces from top downwards. When it is cut open, cut off the hard bit in the middle of each one. Slice the pineapple finely and put into 4 tall glasses with 1 tablespoon of sugar syrup in each glass.

Top each glass with pineapple juice, a little water and stir well, add a few ice cubes in each glass. Wet the rim of the glass and sprinkle with sugar.

Serve with a straw.

ICED COFFEE

Makes 4

4 tablespoons black ground coffee   1 pint boiling water
4 dessertspoons condensed milk   12 ice cubes
4 dessertspoons sugar

METHODS:

Boil coffee with 1 pint of water in a jug, make sure it is quite thick but not too thick. Pour into 4 individual tall glasses and add 1 dessertspoon of sugar to taste. Add condensed milk into coffee and stir well, than add a few ice cubes to the coffee. Serve with a straw.

BARLEY DRINK

Makes 4

8 oz lb pearl barley (225 gm)   2 pints water
8 oz lb sugar (225 gm)

First wash barley and put into a deep saucepan with 2 pints of water. Bring to the boil for about 30 to 35 minutes until it doubles in size and it is very soft. Add the sugar and stir until sugar is dissolved. Leave it to cool.

It can be used as hot or cold drinks. Fill the cold barley drink in a bottle and refrigerate for at least an hour before drinking.

LYCHEE DRINK

Makes 4

Lychees are grown in China. They are exported to many countries. In Malaysia, fresh ones are easy to get from markets and fruit stalls. They taste much better when fresh. The skin is brown and thin and is easy to peel. The inside flesh is white with a stone in the middle. Peel the skin and discard the stone.

16 lychees   4 oz sugar
12 ice cubes   1/2 pint water

METHOD:

First boil 4 oz sugar with 1/2 pint water until the sugar is dissolved. Next cool the syrup. The peel lychees and put a few in a tall glass. Use 2 tablespoons of syrup in each glass and fill wi 3 to 4 ice cubes and stir.

Tin lychees is available in any supermarket.

SOYA BEAN DRINK

1/2 lb white beans
3 to 4 tablespoons sugar
1 pint water

METHOD:

First soak the beans overnight in a plastic bucket. After soaking, the skins of the beans w float on the surface. Throw skins away and rinse the beans out before putting into the blend with approximately 1/2 pint of water.

Add the rest of the water and beans and blend again. Once blended transfer the beans into muslin bag and squeeze out the soya milk, or tie the muslin bag very tight and then let it dr into another bucket.

Once the milk is squeezed out discard the beans which are in the bag. Save the milk and boil with sugar, then simmer for 20 to 25 minutes. Add more sugar if necessary. Once the milk h cooled down, put into bottles and refrigerate. It tastes nice hot or cold.

Malaysian Fruits

FRUITS

There are many varieties of fruits grown in Malaysia and they are very cheap to buy. You can get them from the market stalls or any local shops. Fruit is normally served after meals. Fruit which you could get everyday throughout the year are: Papayas, Water-melons, bananas, pineapples, star-fruits, Jack-fruits and Chinese pears.

The main fruit season comes in the month of June and it lasts for about 3 months. We get mangoes, rambutans, durians, mangoesteens and langsats. Lychees are imported from China.

CHINESE PEARS

Chinese pears are big and round and brown in colour. The skins are very thin and easy to peel. The inside flesh is white, sweet, crispy and juicy. When you bite it, it is crunchy. It is very mouth watering.

RAMBUTANS

Rambutans are red in colour when ripe. The skin is soft and hairy and as big as an egg. You can break it quite easily into half and then you can see the white flesh inside which looks like a miniature coconut. It has a stone in the middle. Do not eat the stones. Rambutans are very sweet when ripe and they grown on trees.

STAR FRUITS

Star-fruits grow on trees. When ripe they are bright yellow in colour and as big as a green pepper. They are very tasty and juicy. Star-fruits can be eaten whole or can be made into drinks by putting them in the blender (sliced).

MANGOESTEENS

Mangoesteens are small round purple coloured fruits. The skins are about half an inch thick. It's flesh is white inside and has a stone in the middle. Some of them have no stones. The stones are edible. Mangoesteens are easy to break open as they are in sections. They taste very juicy.

DURIANS

Durians are big and oval-shaped with green spiky fruits. They are the size of a rugby ball. They grow on very tall trees. When the fruits are ripe, they drop on to the ground. Then the gardener will go round and pick them up by using thick gloves, otherwise he will get pricked by the thorns. Durian fruits are opened from the bottom. A sharp wooden stake is used to split them open into halves and then into quarters. The fruits are in sections. The flesh looks a creamy colour and it has a big stone in it. Do not eat stones. The fruit tastes creamy and quite sweet. It can be eaten with rice or by itself.

PINEAPPLES

Pineapples are grown on small bushes. When fully grown they can be quite big and orange yellow in colour. The skins are a bit spiky. Cut the skins off with a very sharp knife, and then cut off the holes which are left by the spikes. Cut the pineapples into halves and then into quarters and brush them with salt before eating.

PAPAYAS

Papayas are grown on trees. When they are ripe they are big and long and are orange yellow in colour. The skins are thin. Peel the skins off and cut into halves. The flesh is a reddish colour. It has lots of black seeds, discard the seeds. It taste very sweet and juicy. It's another mouth watering piece of fruit. It taste nicer when it's cold. Put it in the fridge to cool.

LANGSATS

Langsats also grows on tall trees. They comes in big bunches. The fruits is small with a light yellow skin. The flesh inside is white and transparent and has a small stone in it. Some of them have no stones. It tastes sweet and sour. The stones are edible.

MANGOES

There are three different types of mangoes. The first one is the round shaped mango which is very sweet. The skin colour is green with a bit of red on it. The second one is oblong shaped and it is quite sweet. The third mango is a big and oval shaped and is sweet and sour. The stone is quite big especially the oblong shaped ones.

JACK FRUITS

Jack fruit is a big oval shaped fruit. When they are opened there are many sections. Each section is as big as a plum and has a stone in it. It is very sweet and the flesh is yellow in colour. It can be eaten as it is, but discard the stones. It can be deep-fried with the stones in it. You can eat the stones once they've been cooked.

EQUIPMENT

A WOK

A wok is a Chinese frying pan used daily in every household or kitchen. It is round and deep, the diameter is 14" - 16" across.It is made from Aluminium or heavy cast iron.

Before using a brand new wok, boil 2 pints of water for about 15 minutes then throw the water away. Then heat the wok with 2 tablespoons of oil till hot, stir it several times. Throw the oil away. Rinse it with hot boiling water each time before use. Never scrub a wok. It will cook better each time it is used.

A wok is used for frying and steaming. Heat gets all the way around the wok so it will not take long to cook the food. Steaming is done by filling it with 2 pints of water and placing a wire tray inside the wok. You place the meat or fish on a metal plate and place it on the wire tray. Cover it with the lid for 10 minutes or more depending on cooking time.

Nowadays there is a modern type of wok which is electric. You cook in it just the same as the other type.

BAMBOO STEAMER

Bamboo steaming is an old fashioned method, but still used daily in restaurants. They come in different sizes and in three or even four layers with a lid. Large ones are used in restaurants, small ones are used in households.

Fill wok with enough water for steaming, keep checking to make sure that the water does not dry up, keep adding water if necessary. Always cover with lid when steaming so that the food cooks quicker. With this method of cooking all the flavour is sealed in the food.

PESTLE AND MORTAR OR STONE POUNDER

A stone pounder is used throughout Malaysia. Every household has one. It is a round vessel made of stone about 6 inches in diameter with a deep hole in the middle. Spices are put into the stonepounder and pounded with the stone handle in order to make a smooth paste. Nowadays electric blenders can be used instead, as a modern alternative.

ELECTRIC RICE COOKER

It is advisable to use an electronic rice cooker which is accurate with it's automatic timer and guarantees that the rice will not burn.

CONVERSION TABLES

Measurements given below are only approximate to the nearest figure. Metric and Imperial measurements must not be mixed. Use only one set of measurements.

Weights

1/2 oz/15g
1 oz/25g
1 1/2 oz/40g
2 oz/50g
3 oz/75g
4 oz/100g
5 oz/150g
6 oz/175g
7 oz/200g
9 oz/250g
10 oz/275g
12 oz/350g
1 lb/450g
2 lb/1kg
3 lb/1.5kg

Volume

1 fl oz/25ml
2 fl oz/50ml
3 fl oz/85ml
5 fl oz (1/4 pt)/150 ml
10 fl oz (1/2 pt)/300 ml
15 fl oz (3/4 pt)/ 450 ml
1 pint/600 ml
1 1/4 pint/750 ml
1 1/2 pint/900 ml
1 3/4 pint/1 litre
2 pint/1.1 litre
2 1/2 pint/1.5 litre
3 pint/1.75 litre
4 pint/2.25 litre
8 pint/1 gallon/4.5 litre

Measurements

1/4 inch/0.5 cm
1/2 inch/1.0cm
1 inch/2.5cm
2 inch/5cm
3 inch/7.5cm
4 inch/10cm
6 inch/15cm
7 inch/18cm
8 inch/20cm
9 inch/23cm
11 inch/28cm
12 inch/30cm

Oven Temperatures

GAS	ELECTRIC
MK1/275 deg°F	140°C
MK2/300 deg°F	150°C
MK3/325 deg°F	160°C
MK4/350 deg°F	180°C
MK5/375 deg°F	190°C
MK6/400 deg°F	200°C
MK7/425 deg°F	220°C
MK8/450 deg°F	230°C
MK9/475 deg°F	240°C

NOTE

Teaspoons and Tablespoons are measured level.

TECHNIQUES

MEAT

The same method applies as for vegetables. Thin strips of meat will take less time to cook. Meat like Pork,Beef or chicken can be cut into 1" cubes but mostly it is cut into thin strips. Chicken meat is sometimes boned, however, Chinese people believe that it tastes better if it is not. Chicken is usually chopped into bite size pieces for cooking.

STIR - FRYING

Stir frying is done in a wok for its quickness. Meat and vegetables are sliced very thin so that it does not take too long to cook. The method is to keep stirring all the time until meat and vegetables are cooked.

STEAMING

Steaming is another method of cooking. It can be done in the wok or a bamboo steamer. Once the food is cooked the flavour is sealed in. Fill the steamer or wok with 1 or 2 pints of water, when it boils place a wire tray across the wok. Put the meat or fish to be steamed onto a metal plate and put onto tray. Cover with lid.

TAMARIND JUICE

Tamarind juice is a sweet and sour fruit. It grows on tall trees, the fruits are brown when ripe and about 12" long. They are sold dried in packets in local Chinese supermarkets. You normally only use about a 2" square for cooking. First soak the tamarind in a small bowl of cold water for 15-20 minutes so that you can get the juice out of the fruit. Squeeze the fruit through a strainer, use only the juice for cooking and discard the rest.

TO DE-VEIN PRAWNS

Prawns have shells on them. Normally these are peeled off with the heads, tails and all the legs. When cooking curry the heads and tails are usually left on because it gives the curry a sweeter flavour. To de-vein a prawn you slit it right up the middle into two halves. Take the grey coloured vein out, then cut the head and tail off before cooking.

VEGETABLES

Different types of vegetables are cut up in different ways. For long green beans you cut it into 2" long lengths. Carrots are sliced cross ways very thinly, piled up on top of each other and then sliced thin again, it should look like it has been shredded. Cucumbers can be sliced across into a 1/2" thickness. For Chinese green leaves you cut it into 2" lengths. Chinese white cabbage is cut into 1" lengths. The whole idea is that the thinly sliced vegetables will not take too long to cook.

TECHNIQUES

CHILLIE PASTE

Chillie paste is made from dried chillies, lemon-grass, yellow ginger, shallots (small onions), blachan (prawn-paste) and garlic. Pound all spices together into a smooth paste. It is now ready for use and will keep in a refrigerator for 1 - 2 weeks.

CHILLIE SAUCE

Chillie sauce is made from fresh red chillies which are put into an electric blender with a little water. Blend into a smooth paste. Keep it handy in the fridge.

COCONUT MILK

Coconuts are normally used fresh. Old coconut kernels (the white flesh inside) that have gone hard can be cut into 4 or 5 pieces and put into a grinder. When it comes out it looks soft and shredded. Mix with a few spoons of cold water and put into muslin and squeeze into a bowl. A thick milk comes out. You can repeat this 3 or 4 times with some more water, each time squeezing the milk into a bowl. Once you have got about one cup full of the thick milk you can then add water to make the amount you need. The coconut can be discarded or you can fry it with some sugar and use it as candy.

DEEP-FRYING

Deep frying can be done in a wok if enough cooking oil is used. Put the meat or fish into the oil when it is hot enough and the temperature is right. The oil can be used again if put into a container when cool and covered with a lid.

GRILLING

Grilling is done over a charcoal fire or a small stove. Fire wood can also be used instead of charcoal. Meat is put onto long skewers across the fire, keep turning them over several times till the meat is roasted. A modern alternative is to use a gas or electric grill. A barbe-cue stove is another method of grilling.

MARINATING

The meat is cut into strips or 1" cubes. It is then put into a casserole dish with spice. Rub spices all over the meat and cover with a lid. Leave it in the refrigerator overnight, the meat will be well flavoured with the spice before being used for cooking. The meat should be left to marinate for at least 3 hours. When the meat has been cooked it will have a lovely aroma and flavour to it.

GLOSSARY

Abalone Fish	Roundish shape fish.
Aji-no-moto	To flavour any soup or vegetable dish.
Aubergine	Long, purple coloured vegetable.
Bamboo shoots	Creamy white look, crispy. Can be obtained in tins.
Beancurds	Made from soya beans, light yellow in colour. Is square shaped and looks like custard. Can be bought fresh from shops.
Bean (soya)	Brownish colour, creamy. Sold in jars. Salted flavour.
Bean (white)	Use for puddings and drinks. Round beige colour.
Bean (black)	Salted spicy fermented soya beans.
Beans (long)	Long bean about 12" long, green in colour very crispy when cooked.
Beansprouts	White shiny, crispy bean. Can be bought fresh or tinned. Can also be grown at home.
Blachan Paste	Made from prawns. Greyish in colour, strong smell, nice flavour.
Bunga Kelatan	A pink curry flower used especially for sweet and sour curry fish. It gives a very nice aroma .
Candle Nuts	Waxy looking nuts known as "Kemiri" in Indonesia. It gives thickness and texture in curry paste. Known as "Buah Keras" in Malaya.
Cardamon Pods	Brown pods have the most aromatic black seeds. Green ones have less aroma.
Cashew Nuts	Shaped like a kidney and when roasted tastes very nice.
Chillies	There are fresh red chillies and green chillies. Can be obtained from supermarkets.
Chillies (green)	Small short chillies are very hot.
Chillies (Dried)	Need to soak in water and drain before use.
Chillie powder	Dried chillies ground into powder. Add to curry depending on how hot you prefer it.
Chillie paste	Made from 5 spices ground together. They are red chillies, prawn paste, lemon grass, yellow ginger, challots.

GLOSSARY

Chinese cabbage White, pale green cabbage. Big bunch.

Chinese Jelly White transparent, looks like white straw. To make jelly, boil in 1 pint of water. Add colouring and sugar to taste.

Chinese leaf Slim looking, greener than Chinese cabbage.

Cinnamon stick Brown coloured stick about 2" long. Used for flavouring curries.

Coriander Seeds Round shaped, beige colour use for garnish curry dish.

Coconut milk Milk from fresh coconut flesh, ground.

Cumin Seeds Beige colour, oval shaped, whole or ground use for curry dish.

Dashi Japanese stock for soup dishes.

Fennel seeds Tastes like aniseed.

Five spice Spice powder, obtained from local shops. Made from five different spices.

Galangal Part of the ginger family, known as Lengkuas or Laos. Can be bought fresh or dried in packets.

Garlic Grows in clusters. It garnishes the food.

Ghee Pure white butter used for Indian curry dish.

Ginger (white) Fresh ginger root. It has a sharp taste.

Ginger (yellow) Yellow in colour. To add to curry spice.

Krupuk Wafer, when fried they are crisp, used as a side dish similar to poppadoms.

Ladies fingers Green finger-shaped vegetable. Can be fried or cooked in curry.

Lemon grass Known as "Serai" in Malaysia. Substitute for lemon juice or lime juice. Use only the bottom 6".

Lime juice Green coloured fruit. Sour taste, very sharp. Squeeze juice before using.

Lychees White creamy fruit, can be obtained fresh or tinned. Sweet taste like coconut.

Mint leaves Green fresh mint leaves, use in soup, curry or as a side dish or garnish.

Mushrooms Dried Chinese mushrooms. Soak in water until soft before using.

Mung Beans A whole green colour bean, which is used for pudding. It is light yellow in the inside.

GLOSSARY

Noodles(egg)	Made from flour and egg. Yellow in colour. You can buy fresh or dried in packets from supermarkets.
Oils	Three types of oil. Peanut, coconut and vegetable oil.
Okras	Known as "Ladies fingers" in Malaysia. Green finger-shaped vegetable.
Oyster sauce	Made from oysters. Very tasty, thick brown sauce.
Peanuts	Salted in packets or raw. It grows in bunches. Available from most shops.
Peppers	Fresh green or red peppers. Red peppers are sweet and the green are spicy.
Prawns	Fresh prawns can be obtained easily from local shops. Tinned prawns are in brine.
Prawns (dried)	Soak in water and drain before use.
Rice (glutinous)	White. Used for puddings and cakes only.
Rice (long grain)	Used for everyday rice dishes.
Rice Noodles	1" wide rice noodles known as "Hor-Fun". Can be bought dried.
Rice Noodles	Another very fine white noodle known as "Tang-Hoon" it has a transparent look and can also be bought dried.
Rice Noodles	A very, very fine noodle known as "Mee-Swar" used for soups. Bought dried.
Rice paper	Paper for wrapping spring rolls. Can be obtained from supermarkets.
Rice (black)	Used for puddings.
Rice Vermicelli	A fine white noodle sold in packets. Known as "Bee-Hoon". Can be used for soup dishes or fried.
Rice wine	A Chinese wine. Substitute for sherry.
Saffron	Looks like orange coloured threads.
Sea-weed	Looks like bunches of straw. Black in colour. Some are small and round in shape. Soak in water till soft and drain before use.

GLOSSARY

Sesame oil	Gives a nice flavour to meat dishes.
Sesame seeds	Gives a rich aroma when roasted on grid till golden brown.
Soya Sauce	Light sauce, made from soya beans. to be used for personal flavour/taste.
Shallots	Small onions which grow in groups. Used quite often in curry paste.
Star anise	Star shaped brown coloured spice. Aniseed flavour.
Star fruit	A star shaped pale yellow fruit. Juicy, used for making drinks.
Sugar cane	Long stems about 6 ft tall. Used for making sugar and drinks.
Sweet potatoes	Long shaped potato used for puddings.
Tamarind paste	Sweet and sour fruit. Substitute for lime juice mixed with water.
Turmeric powder	Ground yellow ginger.
Tow-fu	White square creamy looking beancurds.
Water chestnuts	Fresh or tinned, can be obtained from supermarkets. Fresh ones are very sweet and crispy. Peel off skin before eating.
Yam	Brown coloured vegetable. Peel skin before cooking, the colour will change to purple. Use for puddings or as a vegetable.

INDEX

INDEX

INDEX

INDEX

INDEX